FROM
DARKNESS
TO LIGHT

AF081154

A Novel By:
Sanchari Ghosh

BLUEROSE PUBLISHERS
U.K.

Copyright © Sanchari Ghosh 2025

All rights reserved by author. No part of this publication may be reproduced, stored in a retrieval system or transmitted in any form or by any means, electronic, mechanical, photocopying, recording or otherwise, without the prior permission of the author. Although every precaution has been taken to verify the accuracy of the information contained herein, the publisher assumes no responsibility for any errors or omissions. No liability is assumed for damages that may result from the use of information contained within.

BlueRose Publishers takes no responsibility for any damages, losses, or liabilities that may arise from the use or misuse of the information, products, or services provided in this publication.

For permissions requests or inquiries regarding this publication, please contact:

BLUEROSE PUBLISHERS
www.BlueRoseONE.com
info@bluerosepublishers.com
+4407342408967

ISBN: 978-93-6783-071-0

Cover design: Daksh
Typesetting: Tanya Raj Upadhyay

First Edition: May 2025

Dedication

This book is dedicated to the whole mankind and humanity

Acknowledgement

Love and self realisation are the inspiration for writing this book.

I would like to express my gratitude to "The Book Bakers" literary agency for accepting , editing and representing my manuscript. Sincere thanks to Mr. Suhail Mathur for believing in my book.

I am greatful to "BlueRose Publishers' for accepting my manuscript for republication. I would like to thank Mr. Aditya Singh for helping and guiding me through all the stages of publication and marketing.

And I thank the Almighty for giving me this chance to serve him by dedicating my actions.

Introduction

Naina is a simple homely person who likes to read and study. She likes to speak truth, she believes in love and trust in people. She is not competent in corporate world after completing her graduation.

Tough situations and difficulties of life makes her take shelter at flats of Mumbai where she feels its a home away from home. That is altogether a different world from her early life.

This book is about her journey in a brothel of Mumbai where she loses herself to find herself.

Chapter 1

The women were getting ready for the evening at the hall room, which was boisterous with their cacophony. Their make-up boxes lay open on a few wooden benches. They were brightening their faces with lots of foundation and eyeshades to look like blooming flowers, attracting bees in search of honey.

Bright white lights of the false ceiling were reflecting their images at the wall size mirror as the pageants of some beauty competition. Few of them used very less make-up, yet looked beautiful.

Ishika had become sluggish these days. Her eyes were turning grey like floating clouds burdened with water drops, waiting to flow oozing down the cheeks that were wrinkled. Efforts to cover up wrinkles and brighten eyes seemed to be futile.

"Madam, tea?" Raju, a service boy, came into the hall room carrying a tray filled with small steel glasses of tea.

"Why so late today?" Rianka was annoyed. "Look at the time," she said, pointing at the time on her newly purchased, artificial golden Gucci wristwatch that perfectly matched her gold-sequined red lehenga choli.

"Tea should be served at five. You people never do your work properly," Saloni grumbled.

"Gas cylinder got over while making tea," Raju said as he kept the tray on a bench. "And it took some time to get a new one and fix it."

"Keep quiet! You people always have some excuses handy," Saloni scolded, taking her voice to the highest pitch possible while picking a small glass of tea from the tray.

"Yuck!" She became furious after taking a sip of it.

"Is it tea or something else?" Saloni said irritatingly.

"You always find some fault at everything, madam." Raju said with a smile and went inside the kitchen.

While having tea, they were talking about everything. Many of them liked gossiping a lot. Naina preferred to stay silent and alone, though she was friendly with all of them.

At the hall room, there were a few wooden benches and chairs to sit. Naina took a glass of tea and sat on one of those. The ceiling of the hall was kept purposefully low as there was a hidden chamber above to hide during police raids. A narrow lane that led from the hall to the lounge outside, had air conditioned rooms on both the sides.

Sharma, a tall slim middle-aged person who worked as a manager there, entered the hall in a hurry. "Hey girls, go to the lounge, fast."

Sharma always used to be in a hurry. How fast he would close a deal and go downstairs seemed to be his main motto in life. They used to make fun out of him for such an attitude but he never minded anything; he also laughed with them. Seven people including Sharma, Sanjay, Sunil, and Vinay worked there as managers. They used to stand on the road outside for receiving customers. The brothel was located on the first floor of a three-storied building.

After wearing shoes, the ladies walked along the corridor and lined themselves up at the lounge, which was very well illuminated. In bright yellow lights, all the women used to look so beautiful and gorgeous that sometimes customers used to fall in a dilemma about whom to choose.

Four people in their thirties were sitting on the sofa. They were discussing something between them. Sometimes, they were looking at the women while pointing fingers to someone and again, talking among themselves. One of them was looking at his mobile phone.

Sharma told him, "Sir, please have a look at the ladies."

Then that person looked at them. Sharma introduced them, "From the left side Sarah, Jeni, Nisha, Simran, Sweety, Saloni, Meghna, Rianka, Sheena, Tania, Ishika, Naina, Sofia, Amrita, Vinita, Aarohi, Nafisa and Nikita." He took a little pause, then said, "Tell me, sir."

Ladies were standing like the mannequins in a shop to be savoured by the gentlemen who came there. Sometimes, customers would choose immediately;

sometimes, they would take a lot of time. Sometimes, they would tell them to go back inside, to be called back again soon.

Everybody had their own way of standing and looking at the customers. Nafisa, Saloni, Kajal, Simran, Vinita used to look straight and keep a smile on their face. Sofia, Sweety, Aarohi and Amrita used to look at the floor.

Many times, people used to take woman as per manager's suggestion because they knew, the manager would provide them with someone who would give them the best service. So, everybody tried giving good service to keep her name in the good book of the managers.

"I want that one in the pink short dress," said one of the customers.

"Simran, go inside," Sharma said to her.

Simran went inside.

"I will go with that one in the orange top."

"Nikita, go inside," Sharma said.

"Black dress."

"Sofia, go inside."

Nikita and Sofia both went inside.

"Now you say, sir," Sharma asked the last person.

He was a little confused, his eyes were wandering on them. He said, "Everybody looks good. It's difficult for me to select just one person," he laughed out loud. "If possible, I would like to take them all." He winked at his friends.

"Take all. We are here at your service. Tell me sir, should I send them one by one or you want all of them together in the room?" Sharma laughed too.

The customer widened his eyes. He expressed fear at the idea of taking all the females. His friends broke out into laughter. They started to encourage him. One of them said, "Have the best of fun, buddy. This is one of the best place in Mumbai for having great fun."

"But what will I do with so many? I need to get extra power then," he mocked.

Sharma didn't want to leave this chance to get the best deal possible. He said, "Sir, you have come to my place for the first time, have the ultimate possible fun. Take two girls with you. They will set your mood. You just relax." Sharma's smile became broader.

But the customer seemed to be gentle enough. "I am sure they all are good but I want to go with one person only. You give someone of your choice," he said to Sharma, this time serious.

"Okay sir." Sharma was elated to provide a woman probably with the best service on earth.

"You go with the one in the blue dress, Sir. She is Vinita," Sharma said, "She will give you the best enjoyment that you have not experienced ever. Let me know after you come out from the room. Next time whenever you come here, you'll ask for her. This is my guarantee."

Pride in his voice and smile on face. His words cast a spell on the customer's mind. He looked delighted. "Is it so?"

"Take my words, sir. You will always remember; Sharma has given you some girl."

"Okay, as you suggest; I will go with Vinita."

Vinita smiled at him.

"Thank you ladies, go inside." Sharma said.

***

Naina found her tea totally cold after coming from the lounge. "Do you have some hot teal left in the flask?" She asked Raju.

"Yes, I am just getting it." He got a flask from the kitchen and gave her some steaming hot tea.

"Thanks." Naina smiled at him as she took the glass.

Raju asked, looking at the others, "Anyone else needs tea?"

"Did anyone ask tea from you? Why are you shouting near my ears? Get off," Ishika screamed.

"Madam, I just asked everybody, I didn't ask you anything personally. If you don't need then okay, I am going." Raju walked towards the kitchen.

Ishika took some salt and **turmeric** and went inside the bathroom. Looking at her, Amrita and Rianka exchanged smiles. Amrita said, "Ishika thinks everybody is watching and counting her jobs. So, she is always cautious. Every day, she does something with salt and turmeric to remove evil eye from her."

"She doesn't want to accept the fact that she is aged now, naturally the number of her jobs will wane," Rianka said.

Sweety had all the information of all the females. While making curls in her hair with some gel, she said, "Ishika gives all kinds of wired services that I can't even imagine in my dreams." Her thoughtful comment created pin drop silence in the room.

Sarah tried to protect Ishika.

"Who likes to give all such services inside? She is helplessly doing it to make customers come to her. There is always a pressure of giving good service to the customers, otherwise the manager would replace you at any moment with someone else,"

She said, while mixing glitters in her eyeshades.

Another manager Vinay, a fat and short heighted middle-aged person who would rather describe himself as healthy but not fatty, was present there in the hall, checking a large copy in which the names of the girls, number of jobs, room numbers, etc. were to be recorded. He hardly used to interfere in whatever they spoke. He just looked at them once from the top of his spectacles and lowered his eyes on the copy again.

***

"Simran, Nikita, Sofia, and Vinita go to rooms 2, 4, 5 and 8. Make the customers happy and satisfied. I don't want to get any complaint," Sharma announced as he came in the hall. The ladies were sitting ready with their phones and purses in hand. They immediately went for their work. Babloo followed them for providing room service.

"Sharma ji, same old thing," Saloni scoffed. "Do you ever get any complaint?"

"Yes, sometimes," Sharma said as he stretched his arms up in the air and rested his back on the wall. Maybe he wanted to relax for few minutes after closing a good deal.

"For some complaints of few people, you keep telling it to everybody," Saloni said wryly.

"Not everyone is sincere at work like you. It is my job to remind you and it is your duty to give good service to them. Customers come because of your good service," Sharma said.

"I give good service to make customers and when they come next time, you pass them to the newcomers! Look who is talking about duty. Huh!" Saloni said in a harsh tone. She was a straight forward person who wouldn't exactly talk to please someone.

Sharma didn't take any offence. "Why do you take things personally? I have to take care of everyone, right?"

"And that's on my account—"

"Saloni, shh!" Kajal put her index finger on her lips, signalling Saloni to be silent.

Sharma switched the topic. Looking at Kajal, he said, "You all have only a few years left.

However beautiful you are, the beauty will vanish with time. After a few years, no one will look at your face. So, earn as much money as you can," pointing his finger at Khushbu, Rani and Amrita, he said, "They all have built houses in their hometown."

Khushbu smiled in reply. "It is not easy to build house, Sharma ji," she said, "I am still repaying my home loans."

"Sharma ji, you said it so casually. It was not that easy for me. I could build my own house but it took five long years. I owe the builders still. I am paying them every month," Rani said.

Sharma smiled at her. "You do so much of hard work for the sake of your family. So, don't waste your money; earn and save, so that later you don't regret," he said, this time with a firm voice, "The only friend in this world is money; if you have money, you have everything. I have learnt this lesson from my own life."

"We have learnt this fact from our childhood. Hunger made us adults much before our age," Kajal said.

"Though you understand, still you make mistakes. You waste money on boyfriends, shopping or on addiction," Sharma said.

Vinay finished checking the copy. He said, "The way we earn is wrong. So, we should be honest with ourselves and spend the money for right cause at least. I donate money in temples. I go to the pilgrimages."

"I too feel bad at times. My wife and I had decided not to take dowry for our son's marriage. I am providing them good education; they will earn on their own and take responsibilities. I have a big family to look after," Sharma said.

Sharma used to live in a remote village in Uttar Pradesh. So, taking such a decision was truly appreciable. Sarah cheered him by saying, "You are setting an example; we are glad for you."

Vinay asked for some tea. Sharma went downstairs.

"Ishika was one of the busiest girls here. Every customer used to wait for her to take her service. They would wait hours for her. She didn't even have time to eat food sometimes. Just after coming out from one room, next customer was ready in another room," Sarah said.

Sofia nodded her head. "Those days, she was the most cherished lady here. Even Saloni used to be in high demand."

Remembering her past glorious days, Saloni's face was shining brightly. "Do you remember Sofia, how busy I used to be? I had attained ten customers or more every day." Pride in voice, smile on face.

"We were in competition; who would earn the most in a month? At the end of each month, we compared our diaries." Sofia grinned.

Ishika came out from the bathroom. "My customers still come for me," she added.

Vinay was standing at one corner of the hall, taking a quick sip of tea to finish fast and go downstairs. "Customers are neither yours nor mine. They go wherever they want to go. They have enough money and plenty of options, why would they be yours?" He said, taking the last sip of his tea.

Sarah said, "I have a few customers who keep coming to me from the last seven years or more. They have become my closest friends."

Vinay shrugged his shoulders in reply and went off.

"Huh! They give too much of advice. I've got a headache," Saloni said, looking at Naina.

Now, this was the problem with Saloni, she would love to give advice but won't take it nicely.

Naina, in reply, gave a half smile as she would rather hear all her valuable comments about everything and smile.

"Naina, do you have whiskey pegs in your purse?" Saloni enquired.

"I have two miniatures of sixty ml. But do you have your beer or will you buy?" Naina asked.

"I have two cans now," said Saloni, "My customer came in the afternoon, he gave me." She went in flashback mode.

Saloni loved talking good things about her customers who would buy beers for her and discuss their personal lives with her. Like it happened that afternoon, Saloni was in a deep sleep. No one dared to disturb her while sleeping. But Veena, a kind hearted, charming lady who looked after all the women in the brothel, woke her early in the afternoon.

"Saloni, get up. You have customer." Veena switched on the lights of the room.

Saloni was in a deep sleep, not being able to open her eyes properly, few words came out from her mouth, "Madam, why are you calling me now? What's the time?"

"It is one o'clock."

She opened her eyes a little. "Madam, I don't get up so early. I take sleeping pills. Why are you disturbing me?"

"Saloni, customer is waiting for you. Please get up."

"There are other people, you go and call them. Let me sleep." Turning her face towards the wall, she closed her eyes and covered herself with the blanket to show strong denial for the job. Veena then went near her bed. Sitting beside her, she stroked her hair gently. "Saloni, my sweet heart, get up. Customer wants to take you only. I told him you are sleeping, I requested him to go with some other person but he doesn't want to go with anyone else."

After some time, she removed her blanket. "Okay, you tell him to wait for ten minutes," she said drowsily.

Veena was relieved, "Thank you, Saloni."

"It is alright, Madam. Even I need to work. But the medicine is so strong that it keeps me drowsy till late in the afternoon and you know that," Saloni said as she got up from the bed.

Veena went to arrange a room for the customer. Saloni forgot to ask who the customer was. After some time, she went in the room and was relaxed to see Asif. He never used to take much service. He was a gentle and good person. All her customers knew that she needed beers.

Holding Asif's hand, Saloni said, "Darling, you came so early and woke me up from sleep, so you have to buy extra beers for me now."

Asif looked delighted. "My dear, do you think that I am a miser? Call the boy and ask whatever you want," he said smilingly.

"Today you are in good mood, baby." Saloni placed her hands over his shoulder.

Asif nudged her cheeks. "Whenever I see you, my mood becomes fresh."

Saloni softened. "Really, my darling?" She said, lifting her eyebrows.

"You know how my everyday life is, either busy at office or frustrated at home. The wife and mother keep complaining about each other. Kids don't want to study. Some problems are always there at home or at office," Asif said, letting out a deep breath.

Saloni would have continued talking about her customer if Naina wouldn't have stopped her in the middle of her story.

"So, Asif gave you the beers?" Naina said.

"Yes," Saloni said smilingly.

Naina could see her mood was light now.

"Good, you carry on. I will watch some videos on YouTube."

"Yes, yes, go ahead. You watch your videos. I will call up at home," Saloni said and went to the other side of the hall to talk freely.

Naina, sitting comfortably on a bench with the earphones fitted within her ears, got immediately engrossed in YouTube videos.

***

"Naina Madam," Raju called her name.

Removing the earphones, she looked up at him.

"Madam, customer has come for you. You can directly go in the room. Sharma ji's customer for night," Raju said.

"Customer for night?" She said, pausing the video.

"Yes."

"Which room?"

"Room number three."

Chapter 2

Nikhil, aged around forty, a smart and good-looking man who visited the brothel at least once in three months, was a nice and cool person waiting for Naina at the room. Knocking on the door softly, she entered the room.

"Hi, Naina! Good to see you after a long time, how are you?"

Nikhil smiled as he stood up and shook hands with Naina. There were some people who always gave good and positive vibes and Nikhil was one of them, a man with a golden heart and smiling face.

"I am good Nikhil, how are you?" She smiled too as she kept her purse and phone on the side table.

"I am fine. So, how's life?" He asked as he sat on the bed.

"Life is good. But you can make it better by," after a pause, displaying her best smile she said, "You know that, right?"

"Oh Naina, you and your whiskey." He laughed out loud. "Don't worry; we will have a lot of whiskey tonight."

"Great, you are a true friend Nikhil. Thank you for being so nice to me always." Herv expressions of gratitude were genuine.

"It's not for friendship, Naina," Nikhil said, running his fingers through his hair. "I buy alcohol for you because it makes your mood and sets the ambience. Had I been your true friend," he smiled, looking at Naina straight into her eyes, "I would have done something good for you so that you could have been in a better place than this."

Naina was basically a gentle and polite person who couldn't hurt others and so ended up hurting herself many a times but that too kept her happy and smiling at the end of the day because she took things rather easily and was hardly bothered by so many things.

She smiled nicely at him. "Sometimes, we want to help but we can't go beyond our situation. So, you should not feel bad if you could not help me to live a better life," she said, patting his shoulder, "And if I would have been your true friend, I too wouldn't have engaged myself in illicit sex with you. You know what! We are just two people receiving negative energies from each other, performing negative actions so we both will face the similar opposite negative consequences later."

"Room service, madam." Raju knocked on the door.

Door was open. Raju came inside to serve condoms, towels, tissue papers and water. Keeping them on the side table, he asked, looking at Nikhil, "Do you need anything, sir?"

Nikhil said, "Six large pegs of Teachers, some wafers and cashews."

"Okay, money for the room service and drinks, sir."

Nikhil was taking out his purse to give him money. Raju asked him with a smile, "Diwali bonus, sir?"

Nikhil raised his eyebrows. "Diwali bonus from customer? Is Sharma not giving you anything?"

"Sir, nowadays after the demonetisation, business is totally down but monthly bribes, taxes and other expenditures are still the same. So, he told us to take Diwali bonus from the customers."

Nikhil laughed loud, "Yes, why not! Loot your customers."

Raju melted like butter, started rubbing both of his palms in glee.

"I would have definitely given you tips for Diwali without even asking. I will have to give tips to your Veena madam and others too," Nikhil assured him.

Raju's smile became broader. "Sir, you are our old customer. You have good relations with everyone here so we expect from you," he said.

"That's fine. You may keep the change. Later while ordering food, I will give you more,"

Nikhil said.

"Okay sir, thank you. I am getting your drinks." He went happily.

After Raju left the room, Nikhil said, "Naina, you can make your drink and have. I will take some some time in the washroom. You may order if you need anything."

"Thank you so much," she said.

After some time, Raju came inside carrying a big tray. One by one, he was keeping the drinks and glasses on the table. Naina said, "Raju, can you please open the peg bottle's cap for me?

Sometimes, they just get stuck."

"Okay." He opened the lids. "Madam, lock the door please," he said and went.

She made a drink for herself. Nikhil came out of the wash room. He asked, "Have you finished your drink?"

"I just had one peg, I was waiting for you," she said, "Can I make a drink for you now?"

"Sure, thanks," he said as he sat on the bed.

Naina handed his glass to him. After having a sip of whiskey, he said, "So Naina, you were telling something like we are receiving negative energies from each other. Can you please elaborate? This is something new for me."

Naina wasn't expecting anything like this. But they had the whole night, a lot of time. It's a good idea to discuss things, she thought. Clearing her throat, she began to explain, "We both are in this place in a negative situation. I am here to earn money in an unethical way.

I should have been at home, bringing up children, been someone's wife, doing any other job rather than working as a prostitute. Somehow for some reason after being pushed in this profession, we adjust with the situation. Women basically have a motherly nature. They can't see their family in difficulties, so they sacrifice their life, their happiness and self- respect for the sake of their family or loved ones. This body could have been used to do some constructive work but I am helpless right now, I don't have another option."

She took a little pause and then continued, "You too have come here without telling it to your wife. She knows that you are out of station for some business deal. She trusts you totally and can't even think that you had spent the whole night with someone else and then as if nothing happened, as if everything is fine, you spend your next night with your wife.

"She does not come to know that you actually cheated with her faith and emotion. So, I was telling that we are performing negative actions being motivated by negative desires. My desire to help family is not negative but the way I am helping them; that action is negative. And your desire to enjoy illicit sex is definitely negative."

Naina was little afraid how Nikhil would take her strong words but he seemed to be cool.

"Look Naina, I don't go and sleep with my wife next night after I leave this place. We are married now for fifteen long years. After two babies were born, she totally lost her sexual urges. Later after few years, we both lost our interest in physical relation. I too was busy at my work. Whenever I felt too much stressed, I came here and became relaxed. Sex worked as a stress buster for me. And you know, I am not crazy for service and all."

"You may say having sex is stress buster and physical refreshment but ultimately, it is lust because no love is associated with this physical action. At young age, masturbation was an easy option to be physically released and now you fulfil your sexual desire by coming here.

You actually lose your vital energy in the form of sperms and it will eventually increase your stress level later in life. You should stop losing sperms to live a stress-free life," She said.

Nikhil smiled. "Sexual desire is difficult to control. Ejaculation makes me feel relaxed at times."

"By ejaculating, you waste such a vital fluid of your body. More you keep control on your lust and hold your semen, more creative and positive you remain in life; feelings of love and tenderness stays within you. As you ejaculate semen, feeling of love and positivity goes away and negativity increases."

"You know, I don't come often and also, I don't always come here to have sex. Also you know Naina, it's not possible to have or enjoy a good sex at home due to presence of all the members of the family. There are many restrictions and thoughts like who will think what. That eventually makes sex less interested at home.

Different family values and quarrels within the family members makes sex less interested at home sometimes. So I try to get some fresh air here."

"Yes, that I can understand. In most of the families, the main reason of the unhappiness is the misunderstandings, jealousy and quarrel within the family members themselves. That creates distance within husband and wife making them looking for love and respect outside their own family."

"Naina, I think you have your own thoughts and explanation about life. It's good "

"Actually Nikhil, it all started with self-enquiry. I wanted to know the source of misery and happiness. My journey started with questions like, 'what are the mistakes I have made in life, what I did that I shouldn't have done? Did I hurt someone intentionally? Am I at the right place and doing right thing?' All such queries led me towards knowledge of spirituality.

"I was seeking God and I felt him within so I could tell you all these by the grace of God. Also, I keep watching spiritual videos on YouTube. I have learnt from the speeches of the spiritual masters on YouTube.

"You may listen to 'Bhagwad Gita Asas It Is' by AC Bhakti Vedanta Swami Prabhupada, Sri Shailendra Bharti (Bhagwad Gita), Sri Deep Trivedi (Bhagwad Gita), Jagatguru Sri Kripalu maharaja, Sri Kapiel Raaj (KRS Channel), Sri Bhabajeet Kalita (Exotic Astrology), Mr Ralph Smart (Infinite Water), Sri Gurudev Ravi

Shankar, Sri Abhijit Mishra (Astro Edify), Sri Nitin Kashyap (Astro life sutras), Sri Swami Sarvapriyananda, Sri Jay Lakhani, Sri Deepak Chopra, Sri Radhanath Swami, Smt Pravrajika Divyanandaprana, Sri Sadhguru, Sri Swami Mukundananda, Sri Amarendra Das, Smt BK Shivani, Smt Vanita Lenka, Punneit's Astrology, Nipun Joshi and others."

"Wow! You listen a lot. Fine, then let me hear from you."

"Sure, why not," she smiled.

"Then please explain me in detail about energy and action."

His genuine interest made Naina feel comfortable to talk on spirituality. She began to explain.

"Our whole universe is consisted of energy and matter. Brahman is the all-pervading source of energy, the supreme soul or the Parmatma, the supreme consciousness, a part of the Almighty God.

"All beings are situated in the supreme consciousness. Our body is a dead matter. Body means our gross body and subtle body. Soul is the part of God within our subtle body, which makes us a living being. So, God is present within us as our soul.

"Our gross body is a mechanism consisted of brain, nervous system, sense organs and other multiple organs. Our mind is unconscious about the internal organs and their actions in the gross body. But mind is sub conscious and conscious about the external action of our gross body and subtle body.

"The subtle body is consisted of mind, intelligence, and identity. Intelligence is the ability of putting energy into actions, which means it is our grasping, understanding and decision making ability. Intelligence is the main driving controller, which functions through brain and reflects consciousness within mind.

"Thus, by getting illuminated by the consciousness, the mind becomes aware of our existence. The mind understands that we are 'Jiva' or living beings. The senses start to have different mundane materialistic desires for living in the materialistic plain. The 'Jivas' want to eat, sleep, walk, play and live because the energy is working through the mind and body mechanism to perform actions for living.

"To fulfil those desires, we perform different actions being guided by our intelligence. The law of action is, every action has a similar and opposite reaction. The similar and opposite reaction is our destiny. The cause of action is consciousness, the effect of action is destiny."

"Our mind is unconscious about the internal functions of gross body mechanism but mind is conscious and subconscious about external functions of gross body and subtle body," Nikhil repeated.

"Yes, because that is how we are designed to act in the physical world," Naina said.

"What is soul?"

"Soul is the part of God within our subtle body. Soul is the source of our consciousness."

"Soul is the consciousness and we are also consciousness, right?" Nikhil asked.

"We are soul and we are situated in the supreme consciousness but we cannot call us Eternal consciousness bliss. Only God himself is the eternal consciousness bliss," Naina said.

"Why are you saying so?"

She tried to explain things as much as she could. She said, "Soul is eternal consciousness bliss, a part of God in our heart as a source of eternal bliss. Here you have to understand that I am talking about our own consciousness, which is different in each birth and dependent on the structure of our body and brain mechanism. Our own consciousness is dependent on physical factors and is conditional.

"Our own consciousness changes all the time with different situations of life. But when we elevate our consciousness by increasing Satvik qualities and we practice austerities, then we can feel the bliss and joy within us because the source of consciousness is within us, the soul. Our soul is eternal consciousness bliss. For better understanding you can take the example of light energy; after being reflected onscreen, we see the light. Light is the source of all energy, powerpower, and illumination but it needs a mechanism for us to be able to vsee the light. Our soul is same like light as a part of God within us and our gross and subtle body is that mechanism for the reflection to take place. Our consciousness is the illumination of the light. Until and unless the light is reflected, we will not be able to see the illumination of light."

"Okay, soul is like the light energy and consciousness is like the illumination of that light energy," Nikhil said.

"Yes, and our mind is the screen where every emotion is felt and feelings get featured after we are illuminated by consciousness. Soul is superior to intelligence because it is the cause of our existence and the source of our life force, consciousness, and knowledge within us. Intelligence is superior to mind because intelligence controls and guides the mind. Mind is superior to senses because consciousness is reflected in mind.

"Desires are created in the senses and sense works at the basic level in the body at sense organs. Once the soul enters into a body, it makes it a living being. Our own consciousness is the existing awareness, which gets reflected within our mind through brain mechanism. Our intellect makes us conscious.

"Consciousness illuminates us that we are living beings. The level of consciousness is different for every living being because it depends upon physical factors like how developed our body and brain mechanisms isare. It depends upon how intelligent we are. The more is the intelligence, higher will be the consciousness because the intelligence will be able to grasp and reflect more. To feel the consciousness bliss within, we need to raise our vibrations by performing righteous action," Naina said.

"Who performs all the actions, our own consciousness or the soul?" Nikhil asked.

"Our own consciousness doesn't perform any action by itself. It is an illumination or an enlightenment of our awareness. This awareness is possible due to the functioning of intelligence. Soul doesn't perform any karma. Soul goes through the experiences of our life journey. Our nature performs all the actions by three qualities of it."

"What is nature?"

"Nature is our character. Every living being has its own character and characteristics. We behave or act according to the quality of our character. These three qualities are, Satvik or the quality of goodness, Rajasik, or the quality of passion and Tamasik quality, the quality of ignorance.

"When we have more Satvik qualities in our character, then we perform good, moral and ethical karma. When we have more Rajasik and Tamasik qualities, then we perform selfish, doubtful and negative karma. Rajasik quality keeps us attached with the karma and creates karma bondage.

"The life force within us including our feelings and emotions like joy, anger, hatred, greed, envy, happiness, sorrow, etc. everything is energy. Energy moves through vibration. Jealousy, greed, hatred, sorrow, ego, anger, etc. vibrate in lower frequency. Frequency of emotions like joy, happiness, kindness, honesty, forgiveness is high.

"The more Satvik qualities we have, our vibration becomes higher and we can match with the higher frequencies of the universe, so intelligence can grasp and reflect higher consciousness within mind."

Nikhil was listening quietly. He said, "In the materialistic mundane level, consciousness is restricted within our sense organs only. Nowadays, we seek for sensual pleasure more."

"We indulge in sensual pleasure being motivated by Rajasik and Tamasik qualities of nature. So, our consciousness is low and remains confined within our basic instincts, which makes us selfish. We are concerned only about our own pleasures, own happiness, and our own likings and disliking.

"We are concerned only about our own needs and own requirements. We are bothered only about our own children, own parent, and own belongings. This selfish mentality keeps our energy level in low vibration. Nature performs at the lower materialistic level creating unhappiness and quarrel at home and pushing them looking for relief outside home."

"An intelligent person will have more Satvik qualities in his/her nature, so higher will be the vibration and higher will be the consciousness of that person. Here you have to understand that I am not talking about materialistic intelligence. Here, I am talking about wisdom."

She took a little pause and then continued to talk, "Take tonight's example. You have come here driven by your sexual desire. You wanted to have sex from past couple of days, the basic desire of having sex was created in your senses. We have five sense organs, eyes, ears, nose, tongue and skin. The thoughts of having sex were being featured in your mind.

"But your intelligence controlled your mind that time for few days because you were busy at your work. Tonight, you are here because you made this plan using your intelligence to attain the business deal and a prostitute in such timing, so that your wife does not doubt and your work does not get hampered.

"We desire for pleasure driven by our senses. Senses work at the basic level. We think sensual pleasure will make us happy. But desiring only for the sensual pleasure will keep our mind engaged at the lower materialistic level. Intelligence can control our desires by controlling our mind or it may not want to control.

"But if we have the right knowledge, intelligence can control the mind. Intelligence illuminates our mind with higher consciousness. But you have to understand that consciousness itself is unchanging existing awareness everywhere within and outside us."

Nikhil asked, "If the soul is eternal consciousness bliss within us, then why aren't we conscious while sleeping?"

"Soul itself is eternal consciousness bliss but it needs to be within a physical mechanism to experience life. When we sleep or when we become senseless, then our mind is subconscious or unconscious and brain is in sleeping mode. So, the illumination of consciousness is not taking place within mind. We feel consciousness through brain mechanism. So, we are not physically conscious.

"When people are in coma, the soul is there inside the body but the illumination of consciousness is not happening in the mind physically because the brain is dormant for those activities of the body. But soul exists in our body till we keep breathing.

"The reflected consciousness comes and goes depending on our physical factors. Consciousness can be low and later it can be elevated by practising right 'Samskaras'..' Soul experiences all our actions whether we are awake or sleeping or senseless. While sleeping, we are not physically conscious but due to the presence of soul within the body, the physical actions go on," she said.

"If we are not physically conscious, then why do we dream while sleeping?" He seemed to be curious.

"Not only while sleeping, we dream when we are awake too. Dreams are nothing but the flow of thoughts generated within conscious and subconscious mind. While sleeping, some of our gross body actions (like breathing) keep happening. Same way, some actions of our subtle body like thoughts and ideas appear in subconscious mind as dream. So, we view the things which are there at our subconscious mind as dream while sleeping.

"When we are awake, our thoughts are clear because thought is being controlled and guided by the intelligence. But in sleeping state, our thoughts are vague. Mostly, we don't remember our dreams because brain is not properly active when we are in deep sleep. Sometimes, we remember some dreams of the morning time because our brain is going to be active soon.

"Dreams are the synchronisation of thoughts and daily life incidents while sleeping. A highly aware and sensitive person may dream some upcoming events in advance. This happens because they are aligned with higher frequencies of the universe. Our subconscious mind has knowledge of the upcoming events. A person aligned with higher frequencies of the universe, may observe things of subconscious mind that is going to happen in future in early morning dreams. Soul is always there as the source of consciousness but our mind is unconscious or subconscious when we sleep."

"Sounds interesting!" Nikhil said, "What is your thought on the law of karma?"

"I have already explained that we are not doing something positive, so the outcome of negative actions like indulging in lust, cheating spouse, telling lies, and illicit sex will be negative. This is simple law of karma. But yes, the intention behind any action is a very important factor to be taken in to account while judging any action.

"We do some actions which sometimes may not appear good in the eyes of other people but if the intention is good behind that action, then the result will vary. So, we should not simply judge some action is bad and some action is good in a straight cut way, the intention behind the karma plays a major role in its fruit. The situation in which the action was performed, that is important too.

"I will give you an example, women here are selling their bodies but they are not doing it for their hobby or to become rich or to cheat anybody, they are doing it because there was no other way available for them to look after their family. They are helpless and are being exploited too. Their intention behind illicit sex is not to commit suicide but to live. But it doesn't mean that I am supporting this act, I am just telling you the facts without getting biased."

"So, Naina, what you want to say basically is that there is no straight cut measuring tool to judge karma as good action equals good result and bad action equals bad result, depending on what we think good or bad; our thoughts depend upon how much awareness we have."

"Exactly Nikhil, we the common human beings, don't know which action fructifies in which life time, exactly when and what time it puts us in different situations and produce different intentions in mind. We are not living our lives on this earth from last forty or thirty years, we are living from millions of years.

"We don't know how old we are, our soul lived here from the beginning, we are now and we will be here always. We are soul, tiny parts of the infinite God, so we are also infinite. This present life is only a small particular portion of total past karmas to be executed now. After this particular karma gets executed by our nature using this body, soul then enters in new body.

"Intelligence, mind and identity go with the soul as subtle body. Changing of gross body continues along with the journey of the soul. So, it is our soul's journey what we go through. But our thought is limited within the gross body, so we call it birth and death cycle because we see someone to take birth and die, we just see their gross body to take birth and die. Soul continues its journey along with subtle body.

"We receive positive vibrations from the positive actions. Same way, we receive negative vibrations from negative actions. Energy moves through vibrations. Our intelligence receives this energy. I told you that intelligence is our ability to put energy into action. It is the ability to discriminate between negative and positive energy and use it.

"Intelligence grasps the knowledge and makes us work. Different people may be intelligent In different things depending on their own interest."

"What is the relation between knowledge, consciousness and intelligence then?" Nikhil enquired.

"Knowledge is to know. Consciousness is awareness. Consciousness is nonphysical and is always existing everywhere as Brahman whether you understand it or not. Intelligence makes use of the consciousness for living in this material plain. It reflects the existing consciousness on our mind.

"Intelligence is dependent on our physical factors. Intelligence is physical. Our mind is also physical and our identity is also physical means they are always subjected to change and move as a matter or subtle body. But consciousness is eternal and spiritual."

"This lifetime is only a small portion of our past life actions. Our soul may take millions birth ahead in the future depending on our past and present life karma. Also, the intelligence can be increased in the present life when we practice Satvik qualities and be a devotee of the God."

Nikhil said, "Sounds strange. I have never discussed anything like this with anybody."

Naina smiled. "Do you like what we are discussing tonight?" She asked.

"Yes, I like. Look, I come here to have a good time and relax. I like to have a couple of drinks with someone like you. So many times, I have come and left without even touching their body. You know that, right?"

Naina nodded her head. What he was saying was true. It happened many times that he came, drank and talked and then simply went.

"It is not lust that I crave for," he said. "It's about enjoying drinks in your company. I don't want any female friend, later it may create problem in marriage. This is also a reason I come here and spend some time."

"You seek happiness and pleasure outside, not within. The pleasures you get from the outer factors don last for long. But when you find peace within, that stays with you all the time," Naina said.

He agreed. "So, Naina," he asked, "After soul leaves a body, we think the person died but the soul enters into a different body to perform the remaining balance actions. The past karma will move forward with the soul in its new body and then the body will act according to its physical characteristics of nature."

"Yes, the new body can be of a man, woman, animal, or insect. Now, you understand the reason we are born with a particular destiny. Destiny is the effects and consequences of action. In different situations, how we reacted with what intention that makes our destiny. But we don't know which action will fructify particularly in which life time because we are infinite. The cycle goes on life after life.

"The soul may take birth as a human or animal or insect depending upon our karma to be fructified in the next birth or the soul may exist within the subtle body for years and later, it may take birth within gross body to act in the material plain depending upon the karma. Then depending upon our brain and body mechanism in the next birth, we will experience the reflected consciousness in mind."

Naina took a pause here and said, "Now you understood, soul is the same for all living beings but our own consciousness is different depending upon our karma and physical body."

"Can the destiny of this life be changed with present life time karma?" He asked.

"Apparently it seems, we are studying well so scoring good marks in exams. We think this is present life action. But actually, it was predestined that we will study well and score good marks. We may get married and produce children but this too was predestined. So, what you mean by present life karma is actually how you respond in the present situation depending on your nature."

She continued to speak, "We must perform all our action being detached from any expectation for the fruit of action. We should not desire for the fruit of action because we have our rights only on action. So, we must keep ourselves detached from any kind of expectation.

"Destiny will make us work in that direction. Fruits of action are the toughest mathematical calculations of the universe. So, we better concentrate on our present actions and never stop working whatever may the result be. When we focus on our action other than the result, then we can perform much better because we are focusing only on the action. So, we should perform all our actions keeping God in mind. Then the actions will be righteous, we will be in the path of Dharma.

"I am not telling here righteous action as good karma or bad karma straight away because the definition of good or bad karma depends upon the situations, duty, responsibility and intention. Every action has a similar and opposite reaction. Any action we perform, if it is righteous, the consequences will be right for us.

"If something good happens in life, we know we are getting fruits of good karma, if something bad happens in life, then we know we are paying back our karma. So, in both the cases whether we are in good or bad condition, right thing is happening in our life.

"Whatever is happening in our life is already predestined. When we enjoy good fruits of karma, then we should remain humble and grateful to God. When we pay back our bad karma by suffering pain in life, then also we should remain humble and grateful to God because we are clearing our karmic account by suffering."

"Which God are you talking about, Naina? There are so many Gods in our country."

"I am talking about Lord Krishna, the supreme almighty, the ultimate absolute truth to be known. But sadly, we are running behind illusionary, superficial materialistic desires, which keep our nature trapped in illusion lives after lives.

"We forgot the real purpose of our soul taking birth. We get to be born as human beings after many births; we should not waste our birth by attaching ourselves with the bondage of karma. The Rajasik qualities of our character keep us bound with karma and we keep taking birth again, and again to pay them back. When we work selflessly, then soul does not get karma bondage.

"If we remain stable whether we get good or bad result of any action, then also we can avoid the bondage of karma. We get human birth to enquire about God, to be a devotee of the god to receive his grace. We get human birth to get self-knowledge to attain Moksha."

Naina had to stop on hearing a soft knock on the door along with a voice telling, "Sir, you were supposed to order food." It was Raju reminding them for food.

"Yes Raju, come on in." She opened the door for him.

"Sir, what should I order?" He asked, looking at Nikhil.

Nikhil looked at Naina and said, "You may order whatever you wish to eat. I would like tobhave something light, like pizza maybe."

"Good, even I like pizza, thin crust vegetable pizza which we both can share," She said happily.

"Are you sure? Don't you want to eat anything else?"

"Yes, sure," Naina confirmed.

Then Nikhil looked at Raju and told him, "Raju, can you repeat the drink order, please? Once the pizza comes, you get all of them together."

"Okay sir. Madam, you can lock the door." Raju left.

"Naina, you can order from your mobile phone. Don't you want to try anything else?"

"Okay, I will order for some desserts too."

"Good. You place the order first."

She called up the nearby pizza delivery centre and ordered the food. Then she told, "Thanks that you have repeated the order for drinks but I don't want to drink anymore now. Three were enough for me."

"Oh really, that's great!" He looked delighted, "No problem; you can keep them. But I would like to know what happened suddenly that you don't want to drink. Whenever I met you, having five or six pegs was nothing for you."

"Actually Nikhil, tonight we are discussing about spirituality. It will be difficult for me to think and speak if I am drunk. Alcohol does not let us think or act wisely. It has a direct negative impact on our emotion. Sometimes, it excites the sense and then the intelligence loses its control over mind and then we perform wrong actions. I have realised it," Nainav admitted.

He smiled, "I am really happy that you at least got a control over your drinking. I never insisted you on drinking but you told me that after drinking, you feel comfortable and can give better service."

"Yes, I drink to remain absorbed within myself. But for most of the people, it is difficult to remain wise after drinking. Most of the women drink here. You know why?"

He said casually, "They drink to give good service so that customers keep coming here regularly and the business goes on."

"That is of course there, that is the reason to justify the kind of service we give, to justify drinks. Without drinking alcohol, it is really difficult to feel comfortable. It is really not that easy to remove all the clothes and give service to a completely unknown person for money. It is the most difficult job for any woman.

"A woman is a mother by nature; she wants to be a wife and a mother but not a prostitute. She is a mother, a wife, and a daughter so she sells her body to feed her family, to take care of her family, she sacrifices her decency.

"Women do it helplessly because once they are pushed into prostitution by any situation of life, they can't come out easily. They are trapped in the world of falsehood. In the beginning when they earn money, help family, do shopping, eat good food, take care of the family, they feel good.

"After some time, the joy goes away while facing the hard-real practical situations of life. Then they want to run away from this illusionary false world but by that time, all the roads are blocked. Alcohol gives numbness to the nerves, so bearing the pain of being touched by so many different people, becomes a bit easier."

Nikhil kept quiet. He was in deep thought. Taking a deep breath, he said, "I understand, it is not your hobby to sleep with so many different people. So many customers come here lonely, depressed but full of wealth. They don't have happiness or peace in mind. They come here to buy happiness for some time.

"People think that women in this profession deliberately choose this profession to earn money and have sex. But in reality, it is not the case. Though some women may work as call girls or prostitutes for earning extra money to become rich or to have fun too but they don't come to work in a brothel.

"In a brothel, we generally meet those women who came in this profession when prostitution was the last option for them. Naturally, you people are also not happy. Then what is happening here?" He asked seriously.

"In reality, you are buying miseries for life by coming here to fulfil your lust. Because once you choose illicit sex to fulfil your lust, later you don't try to control your negative desires.

Women drink alcohol to make themselves comfortable with the situation so that they can feel and act happy in front of unhappy customers to show them a false gimmick that everything Is so sweet like candy.

"Girls lie and act happy in front of customers to create an illusion of happiness to make

them feel good. They have no other way too because that is what they get paid for. Customers are also cheating their wives, girlfriends; they too lie and try everything to get the best service and waste semen, such an essential fluid that has the energy of creation. Consciousness becomes low as you keep losing semen."

Nikhil kept quiet.

"Just think Nikhil, where we all are going? We all are moving towards total darkness," Naina said, "We live in superficial materialistic false gimmicks. We have no control over the senses. We are surrounding ourselves with unreality and falsehood. We are telling lies most of the time to the most of the people.

"We entangle ourselves into such superficial illusion in search of pleasure and happiness. We are the product of our thought, so it is high time to analyse ourselves andvour actions. We should start self-analysing to know the self."

"Self-analysis, I never heard about it. I remain too busy in my office work. The most of my life is busy in the calculation of profit and loss analysis."

"Profit and loss analysis of money or happiness in life?"

"Money and happiness are two sides of the same coin nowadays. To analyse profit and loss of my business, I am losing the profit of my life, I guess. What were you telling about self-analysis?" He enquired.

"Well, when you analyse yourself, when you enquire about yourself, then you start your journey within to know yourself. Once you know yourself, then you realise what false ego is," she said.

"Naina, what is false ego? As far as I know, ego is pride."

"Ego is self-identity. When we nurture our identity with deep satisfaction and gratification, then our identity becomes our pride. When we identify ourselves with our body, name, fame, status, etc. that identification is called false ego. If I ask you your name, you will say you are Nikhil.

"You are an entrepreneur from Ahmedabad. But in reality, now you know, this is your identity only for this life time. You are carrying your past lives identities in your subtle body in this life too. Remember, I told you our subtle body consists of mind, intelligence, and ego or the identity.

"In your next life, you will be someone else, a new name, new body, maybe some other animal or insect or bird, we don't know. In reality, you are a soul. Soul is the only absolute truth a part of Lord Sri Krishna inside all of us. Rest everything around us is illusion. Our body is a dead matter.

"Our nature, our surroundings, everything is changeable, everything is continuously changing its forms, looks, colour, identity, smell. Nothing is permanent. Everything is perishable. It is only the soul which does not perish or change because it is the part of God inside us.

"We had already discussed; soul enters a new body after it leaves its old costume to payback some old karma. When we come to know the real truth that we are soul and our identity is physical and matter of change, then we don't attach ourselves with our name or fame. We use our identity for external use in our society, locality, office, within friends, relatives.

"But internally we know, this present physical identity is temporary and only for this life time. So, we don't engage ourselves in any action to fulfil or boost our ego or pride. We remain humble throughout our life."

She had to stop because Raju was knocking on the door. "Madam, I got the drinks and the pizza both," Raju said from outside.

Chapter 3

"Thanks, Nikhil, for the exclusive dinner," Naina said, sitting comfortably, keeping a pillow on her lap.

"Pleasure's all mine," he said, smiling. "Tell me, Naina. What is spirituality? What kind of realisation is that? What do you exactly mean when you say some one is spiritual?" Nikhil said, getting back to the topic.

"Spirituality is the non-physical part of a being; which is a part of Brahman. Other than the Brahman, everything else is Maya. Brahman interact with Maya with the three qualities of character, namely Satvik qualities or the qualities of goodness, Rajasik qualities or the qualities of passion, Tamasik qualities or the qualities of ignorance. Actions are performed by our nature according to its quality. So, all our actions are actually being performed in the mundane level of Maya.

"The birth and death cycle and our actions are continuously going on in the mundane materialistic level of Maya. We should not be deeply affected by these actions. We should try to remain stable in sorrows or in happiness because the cycle of birth and death, sorrows or happiness, all other actions are being performed by us since infinity and these activities will keep happening.

"We should not be worried by the flow of action. The more Satvik qualities we have, higher is our vibration to match with the higher frequency of the universe. The higher is the frequency; the better is our intelligence to understand Brahman and Maya.

"When we enquire about God, then we realise that Lord Krishna is the source of our consciousness, joyjoy, and happiness. Only Lord is the eternal consciousness bliss. But our own consciousness is reflected, limmited, and conditioned by physical factors and karma. When we realise this truth then we become devotee of the lord.

"We realise that we all beings are equal for God. All living beings are having the same soul within them. So, we can feel the oneness with the whole creation of God. This realisation of oneness with the whole creation of God is called spirituality. Spirituality makes us peaceful from within."

"What is Brahman?"

"Brahman is the all-pervading source energy, supreme soul, the eternal consciousness bliss, a part of Lord Krishna."

"Isn't Brahman the absolute truth?"

"Yes, it is the absolute truth."

"Then why are you telling that Brahman is a part of Lord Krishna?"

"Lord Krishna is the creator, maintainer and knower of the Brahman and Maya. So, Brahman is a part of him. When we attribute the qualities of character in Brahman to worship, we call it Saguna Brahman. When we worship Brahman as the supreme soul and without the qualities of nature, then we call it Nirguna Brahman.

"When we have a physical body and we act under the qualities of nature keeping ourselves limited within certain characteristics, then it is really difficult for us to worship Nirguna Brahman and understand it as well. A yogi who acts beyond the qualities of nature and overcome the limitation of characters can understand Nirguna Brahman.

"Character or karma nothing can bind a yogi. A yogi being in the 'Samsara',,' remains free from all the bondage of 'Samsara'."

"So, a yogi is not under the law of karma or the law of nature?"

"A yogi is also under the law of karma and the law of nature till the soul exists in yogi's physical body. But yogis are enlightened and liberated being. They are free from the attachment of samsaras ."

"Then how will I practice spirituality?" Nikhil enquired.

"You have to start with self-enquiry. You look within yourself, analyse your own actions in different situations. Thus, you become an observer of your own action. Learn to perform your own duty as your Dharma. Dharma is the eternal and inherent nature of reality, the path of righteousness. You have to increase qualities of goodness in your nature like kindness, honesty, truthfulness, forgiveness to raise your vibrations.

"Do Pranayama through which you can control your breathing to channelise your life force.

Controlling your mind from different desires and concentrating on Lord Krishna may seem to be difficult at starting but with regular practice and detachment, you can do it. Yoga is a way to be united with the divine bliss.

"You can read the 'Gita';;' you may keep in touch with spiritual people to acquire knowledge about Lord Krishna, about our scriptures and to discuss about 'Gita,' astrology and humanity for the guidance towards self-knowledge and inner fulfilment. Keeping ourselves attached with spiritually elevated people help us to be on the right path.

"Doing superficial worshipping to the Lord, with desire or greed in mind for the mundane materialistic things like money, car, house, promotions, etc. will keep us attached more in Maya. And we will remain entangled within the bondage of karma.

"Our nature is the doer. We perform karma according to the quality of our nature. So, when we start self-analysing, we need to start with our nature first. How do we respond in any situation, are we having more Satvik, Rajasik or Tamasik qualities in us? We all have all the three qualities within us.

"God of Satvik quality is Lord Vishnu. God of Rajasik quality is Lord Brahma and the God of Tamasik quality is Lord Shiva. They have three different qualities for the purpose of creating, maintaining, saving, and destroying the creation and again to recreate."

Nikhil asked, "We do actions because we have some desires. The quality of our nature produces desires in us. So, behind any action it is very natural that we will have some desire.

"If we don't desire the fruits of action, will we not lose our interest in karma?"

"An ignorant mind has more desires. When consciousness is elevated, desire is less. We should not desire for the fruits of karma, as I explained, we are old soul living here from the

millions of years. The actions we are performing and the result of that is already predestined. You will get the fruit according to your destiny and perform action according to the destiny. The only thing we can do is to respond wisely and perform our action in a positive way because the way we respond in a situation, becomes our present action.

"For an example, you are trying to clear UPSC exams from last five years but ultimately, you couldn't clear it. You got disheartened, later you got a job of a teacher in a school. You became a school teacher because you had it in your destiny that you will be a teacher. But the karma you performed while preparing for the UPSC exams, will also not be wasted.

"Your efforts, your knowledge will not go waste. Later in future, you may become a professor in life. The knowledge, efforts, persistence, patients which you have acquired while preparing for UPSC exam, shaped your nature. Also, in future life times, you may take birth as a very knowledgeable person, you may clear any exam in the first chance because these qualities get carried forward in your next life with soul.

"Every action has the similar and opposite reaction, nothing goes waste. Every action gets fructified now or later. There is no point to expect any fruit of our action but to perform karma as our duty, as our Dharma. When we realise this truth, then we don't get disheartened even if we do not succeed after doing hard work.

"Everything happens in perfect mathematical calculations. This mathematical calculation is called astrology. Our present horoscope is our karmic account balance sheet of past life karma. We are born with our destiny to go through different situation, the way we react at the situation, makes our future destiny."

"True, when we learn such knowledge, we understand the truth of life. Then we can cope up with different situations without being dishearten. We learn to live life with positive attitude.

Naina, tell me one thing, don't we have free will to act?" He asked.

"The concept of free will is an illusion. Free will is an illusionary truth. Destiny and free will are like two sides of the same coin. Destiny is the ultimate truth and free will is an illusionary truth at the mundane level of Maya. You can understand and realise things as per your own perception."

"What? I didn't get you."

"Free will is our choice to respond in any situation. Free will works through our subconscious mind. What we respond in a particular situation is decided much before within subconscious mind by the intelligence. We do that what is already decided within our subconscious mind.

"But our conscious mind is not aware of that decision. So, we think superficially that we are acting freely. What is decided within our subconscious mind, that decision is taken based on the quality of our nature."

"Why did you say, free will is an illusion?"

"At the physical level we think we have free will and we do everything as per our own wish. This is how our consciousness gets reflected at the physical world that we work according to our free will. But the real truth is, we are the cosmic energy performing actions since ages under planetary control. What is above that is below. We act under the law of nature and the law of karma."

She gave him an example to make things clear. She said, "You are the boss in your office. How much free will do your employees have in your office?"

Nikhil said, "There is regular routine job, which is already pre-decided and programmed for most of the employees. Their free will is not needed. But yes, what are they having for lunch or talking within them personally, etc. is not my concern."

She said, "Same way, we too are programmed and destined to perform karma according to our nature. In your office, employees are designated to perform according to their post and position. No one is free to decide anything on their own without your knowledge and going against the office rules. Again, your will is dependent on market and clients, etc.

"Same way, we too are destined to perform our respective karma. You said that you are not supposed to be concerned about their personal matters but someone else or some other person is concerned about their personal matters because those actions of their personal lives are related with those people; different department of the 'samsara'..' There also we are not free.

"We are conditioned and bound by karma. We are motivated to act according to our nature. Thus, we all are functioning under the universal cosmic law. Even the movements of planets are also regulated and calculated. Everything is happening in mathematical order. You think, if the moon or the planet earth starts to move freely on their own, what will be the consequences?

"Different energies of planets are guiding and affecting us in different directions of our life In a balanced and calculative manner to make us work in certain direction. Lord Krishna is the supreme almighty. He is our creator, father, dearest friend, and guru. The nature is our mother.

We are worshipping God in temples but not educating our mind with right knowledge. The desire for the pleasure of our senses and our ignorance is the cause of our sufferings."

"So, Naina, what you want to say, we suffer our own deeds. But all these sufferings are at the materialistic mundane level when we are in the grip of the Maya. The ultimate truth is that, we keep taking birth, perform action and die, taking birth, perform action and die; thus, the cycle of birth and death goes on in the materialistic mundane level of Maya, soul remains unattached from action," Nikhil said.

"Absolutely, you know Nikhil, astrology is the divine spiritual science which explains the karmic cycle we are born with in this present life time. Astrology is a part of the Vedas.

People have misconception about astrology that it will change our destiny and luck by remedies and gemstones. No, it doesn't happen like that.

"Astrology is the mathematical calculations of our karmic account. We are born to act according to our karmic account as calculated in the birth horoscope. Horoscope is the map of the journey of our soul. I told you earlier, that the calculation of karma includes situations, intention, duty, and responsibilities.

"Saturn is the planet of action; Saturn has our karmic account. Saturn is the judge. We are born with a particular ascendant due to our past life karma to be executed in this life."

Nikhil said, "So, is this the reason people are so scared of Saturn? People always do so much of worship on Saturdays, offer oil in the temple on Saturday and keep fasting on Saturday to get blessings from Saturn."

"Yes, we do everything except what we are supposed to do. We do not change internally as human beings. Saturn is the planet of discipline, action, hard work, duty, commitment, sacrifice, limitation, restriction, structure, and dedication. We should imbibe all these qualities within us to improve ourselves.

"We must be sincere and disciplined at our works, must take responsibilities and must behave well with subordinate because Saturn represents servants. We must show gratitude and respect to the older because Saturn represents old age people. We should be kind and helping towards handicapped people because Saturn represents handicapped people. We should be kind to poor people because Saturn represents poverty.

"We wear iron ring in middle finger or blue sapphire to correct the problem of Saturn. We think there is some problem in our horoscope, Saturn is creating problem and we need to rectify Saturn. Saturn is like the report card. It is not possible to change the marks on the report card; the possible thing is to work hard to get a better score next time. As I explained, actions will go on, not to be worried by the flow of action.

"Saturn gets exalted in the sign of Libra, meaning Saturn is the happiest when he is in Libra sign. Libra is the seventh sign and sign of balance, sign of other people, partner, market, business. Saturn gets its directional strength in seventh house. Seventh house is the house of partner, other people and business.

"It means, Saturn is most comfortable in the sign of balance and partnership, it means we should be respectful while communicating with other people or with our partner. We don't do that, instead we fight with other people or with the partner, we insult other people and our partner, we cheat other people and partner. Then we expect good result of our karma.

"People offer oil to Saturn temple because Saturn represents iron, oil, etc. anything we extract from beneath the ground. Saturn represents all the heavy industries and factories etc. It is easy to offer oil, easily available in the market but bringing change within us is tough. So, we go for easy solution.

"When people enter within the mines to excavate iron ore or gemstones, how much difficulty they face. We don't realise their pain but we run after the gemstone to change Saturn.

Saturn represents labours, farmers and all the hard-working people of the society. Unless we change our thoughts and behaviour towards them, our life will not improve."

"How to feel the presence of God?"

"God is omnipresent, he is within us and he is everywhere," Naina said, "I will give you an example. When you take a photograph of your friends or family using the back camera of your mobile phone, you will not be seen in the photo. But you know you were present there that time, you only clicked the photo but you are not being seen in that photograph because you were just on the opposite side of the people to take the photo.

"Your friends and family are the part of your existence. Because of your presence there, the presence of your friends and family in the photo was possible. You are present within them in their mind; your kids have your DNA. But still, you are aloof and different from them as a whole being. Being within them, you are not them. You are a different entity altogether on the opposite side of the photo.

"When someone else sees this photo, he/she will not see you in the photo but he/she may know that you are the cameraman. The photograph is your creation, capturing the light energy through a particular mechanism called camera. The photograph is nothing but an illusion or the Maya. The creator of Maya is not a part of it but is present there because he only created the Maya."

Nikhil seemed to be quite amazed. Then he looked at his watch and said, "Look at the time, I have to go now. This place closes at four am, right?"

"Yes, but you can sit for some more time if you wish to take some rest."

"No Naina, I should leave now. I really had a good time because we discussed the most important knowledge of life about which I was totally unaware."

She smiled at him. "Thank you."

"After discussing such topics, I am feeling like something is changing within me. I am more inquisitive to know about Lord Krishna and the 'Gita'."

"You really made me smile from the bottom of my heart," she said.

He looked at his mobile again, "I have to rush."

"Are you going back to Ahmedabad now?"

"No, I am going at the hotel," he said, "I have meetings in town in the afternoon."

"Oh, okay. Bye then. Take care and have a good sleep," Naina said.

"You too take care, Naina. Bye." He opened the door and went.

Chapter 4

"I was waiting for you, Naina. Have you got your whiskey?" Saloni asked eagerly as soon as Naina entered the inside hall.

"Of course, yes. Let's go and sit in your room," Naina said.

"Cool, I have two cans for now," Saloni said.

Both were beaming because soon they were going to have some relaxed moments. No one would call them for any work now and they could sit and enjoy some leisurely time. They went to Saloni's room. All the rooms were almost similar. The bed was at one side, there was an attached cupboard with the wall on one side of the bed.

Saloni sipped at her chilled beer that she just exchanged with the warm one. Naina poured some water in her glass.

"Naina, do you want some wafers?" Saloni offered.

"No Saloni, thanks. You can have. Shall I play some music?" Music was a must while drinking.

"Sure." Saloni liked music too.

"Naina," Sofia was at the door, "How was the customer?"

"Customer was very nice. But why are you standing there? Come and sit," Naina said.

Sofia came inside and sat beside her.

"Will you take some beer?" Saloni asked her.

"No, my dear, you know I drink only when I am at work. Otherwise, I don't." Then she looked at Naina and asked, "Were you with Nikhil?"

She was about to reply but then Ishika entered the room. "Hey! What's going on?" She said,

while removing her make-up with a cotton ball.

"Nothing much, you can see," Saloni said.

Ishika asked Sofia, "Were you saying something? I interrupted you; I think." Throwing the cotton ball in the dustbin that was placed at one corner of the room, she sat on the bed.

Sofia said, "I was talking about Nikhil. He is a very nice person. I had been with him before."

"But how do you know Nikhil came?" Naina asked her, surprised.

Sofia took a pillow on her lap. Placing both of her hands on the pillow, she sat comfortably.

Sofia talked and they listened in silence.

***

"I was in the lounge in the evening to have a talk with Veena madam. No customer was there.

Nikhil entered the hall at that time," Sofia said.

They had both stopped talking and looked at him. Nikhil smiled at them. Veena greeted him cheerfully. Sitting on a sofa, he said, "How are you, Veena madam? Is everything fine?"

"It's not fair, Nikhil. When you come here, then only you enquire about me. Otherwise, you never call up," Veena said, displaying some fake emotions.

Nikhil laughed loud. "Madam, already my life is so hectic and busy that I hardly get time for myself. When I come for a business trip, then only I come here," he said, "Otherwise trust me madam, I don't have time to think about anything else."

"Yes, you are very busy, I know." Veena came back to normal mode. "How's your family?"

"All are good, busy in their own world," Nikhil said. Looking at Sofia, he asked, "Did you go to Calcutta this year for your Durga puja? That is the best festival there."

"I went for the festival. But I didn't enjoy much. The city was too crowded and environment was so polluted with fire crackers and all kinds of noise," Sofia said, irritated.

Veena too agreed. She too, was from the same city. "Very true, during Durga puja festival they make big kiosk. Sometimes, they block the main roads and other lanes. All the people of the city come on the roads," she said, "Even during Ganapati festival in Mumbai, same thing happens."

"But that's how these festivals are meant to be enjoyed for those few days," Nikhil said.

"Enjoyment, fun! Maybe," Sofia said, "But I've felt something else."

"What?" Nikhil asked.

Clearing her throat, Sofia said, "Me along with my family were standing at a queue for a visit to Maa Durga. It took more than two and half hours to reach her inside the kiosk. There I saw they had dumped so many garlands, coconuts, sweets, etc. in a corner and as if those were extra or not needed anymore.

"There were so much of lights and decoration inside. Some big company invested so many gold ornaments on Maa Durga's idol to be displayed. For that also, the crowd was more."

"People's eyes were on the gold ornaments," Nikhil laughed.

"Yes, then listen." She took a little pause and continued, "As I came out from the kiosk, I saw few handicapped, old people and children were begging food outside, they were hungry.

Inside the kiosk, too much of light and decoration and the things were getting wasted but outside the kiosk, there were starving people in the darkness. This thing touched my mind and squeezed my heart."

Nikhil and Veena kept quiet.

"You know what I actually found funny!" Sofia said in a light mood.

"What?" Nikhil was inquisitive.

"They have categorised people into VIP, VVIP queue. Rich people were treated specially to see the idol of God soon with VIP pass. Poor or middle-class people could see the idol of God later. In front of God, we people are tagging ourselves as VIPs."

"Water, sir," Raju entered with a glass of water on a tray.

Nikhil took the glass from the tray and drank the water.

"Thanks, Raju." Keeping the glass on the tray, he said, "Where is Sharma? Call him, please."

"Sir, he is there in the lane below. He might not have seen you. I will just call him."

After Raju went downstairs to call Sharma, Nikhil looked at Sofia and asked, "Would you

mind anything if I go with Naina tonight?"

"Absolutely not Nikhil, you may go with anyone you wish. Have a good time." Sofia smiled.

***

Saloni took out another can of a beer from her cupboard. She jostled her face as she sipped at the warm beer.

"You could have exchanged the warm beer with a cold one," Naina said.

"That's fine. I'll just get some ice from the kitchen," Saloni said. She got down from the bed and wore her slippers.

Vinita came in the room looking for Saloni that time. "Hey Saloni!" She asked, "Do you have some hash?"

"Hmm." Saloni took out some hash from a secret chain gap of her purse. "I always keep some hash in my bag. One of my customers gives me," she said.

"Thanks." Vinita grinned, "I knew I'll get it here, mine got over."

"Roll one for me too," Saloni said as she walked towards the kitchen.

Vinita took out a newspaper from her purse and spread it on the bed. Then she took a safety pin and stuck the stuff on it and heated it for few seconds with a lighter. Mixing the stuff with tobacco, she rolled few joints. Vinita lit up a joint and filled the room with smoke. The smell brought Sarah from the other room. "Hello girls, have you all seen the time? It is almost five thirty now. Won't you all sleep?" She said, raising her eyebrows.

"Hey Sarah, sit. What were you doing?" Ishika said and shifted a bit to make place for her.

Sitting beside Ishika, she said, "I was talking to Akash."

Ishika asked her, "What did he say? When are you both going to settle?"

"Don't ask me, Ishika. I ask the same question to him. He keeps telling me to wait for few days and that day never comes," Sarah said, letting out a deep breath of frustration.

"You helped him start his own business, you gave him money," Saloni said, mixing some ice in her beer.

"I tried to help him as much as I could," Sarah said, while biting her lips to control herself from crying.

Ishika tried to switch the topic. "How's uncle and aunty?" She asked.

"Maa and baba are not keeping well."

"Who is at home to look after them?"

"My brother is at home nowadays taking care of them," Sarah said, "Though my younger brother takes care of them but I only bear all the expenses. He recently finished his engineering."

Vinita inhaled a lot of smoke and held it inside for quite a long time before releasing the smoke.

"Good to hear that your brother's studies are over, you are much relieved. But why is Akash doing like this with you?" Saloni came close to Sarah and asked.

"I don't know, Saloni. Nowadays, he avoids me and how can I force someone to have a relationship with me? I work as a prostitute but I do that for living. Akash knows everything about me. He met me here only." Sara's eyes filled with tears.

"He was Nafisa's customer," Sofia said.

"Yes," Sarah said, while trying hard to swallow the lump in her throat. "But when we met, we fell in love. But now his mind is changed." Tears rolled down her cheeks.

"Our life is a curse. We are born to help people in exchange of our body and self-respect. No one will ever know the story behind."

Vinita was listening quietly. Now she said, "I still remember the first day when I slept with customer for the first time in my life, not here but in Calcutta."

"What happened there?" Ishika asked.

"I went to a hotel in the afternoon." She took little pause and said, "I was so nervous and feeling so low about everything. That person understood my dilemma. He made a large peg of whiskey and gave me to drink. I had the first peg. After that, I made up my mind and did the job."

"So, whiskey made it easier for you," Saloni said.

"At that moment, of course it did. But later at night, I was not able to sleep. I was feeling like a snake was moving on my body. I opened my eyes with fear. I cried and spent so many sleepless nights. I could not even touch that money for some days," Vinita said,

"Whatever I bought with that money kept reminding me of those moments, making me ashamed of myself."

"Vinita, you wanted to open a beauty parlour, you were telling," Saloni said.

"Yes, I see that dream quite often that I have a beauty parlour. I am working hard for my own parlour but I don't know when my dream will come true."

Chapter 5

Entering her room, Naina saw Manisha was listening to music in her phone, lying on the bed. The purple colour dim light was on in the room.

"Hi, Manisha! How was your day (night)?" Naina asked as she switched on the lights.

It was six-thirty in the morning, their usual time for sleeping.

"Not bad. I got four customers tonight but I needed six at least, you know? Next week, I will have to send a good amount of money home," Manisha said as she put off the music.

"Is there something serious?" Naina asked as she kept her purse and phone on the bed.

"Nothing serious but my father is buying some land for farming in the village. Half the money is already given to the land seller. Rest I have to pay in the coming months."

"Oho, okay," Naina said and opened the cupboard to take out her night dress.

"My father takes tension for me," Manisha said. "He says I should buy some land for future security."

"Hmm."

"You know, I called up Ramesh in the evening but he didn't come. He gives good tips and not only that, he even sends all his friends to me."

"Don't worry, he will come tomorrow."

Manisha turned to the other side and closed her eyes.

***

"Naina madam, Manisha madam, get up please," Babloo said as he switched on all the lights of the room. He had got a small tea tray with two glasses of tea on that. Naina got up and took the glasses.

Manisha was still sleeping. She never minded having cold tea.

"Thanks, Babloo," Naina said, "What's the time now?"

"Two-thirty pm," Babloo said and went.

They used to sleep keeping the door open because anytime they might have to get up to attend customers. Though their work timing was from four pm to four am, still customers could come anytime. Few people came really early in the morning like at seven or eight am.

Naina took a little sip of tea. It was refreshing. She took out her mobile that she kept beneath her pillow. The whole building was quiet. No one was talking over the phone or laughing loudly on some silly jokes. The noon felt peaceful.

Playing a soft mantra chanting on YouTube, she took out her bag from the cupboard. Thinking what to wear that day, she selected a dark green top and denim shorts. She took out her toothpaste, brush, face wash, body wash and body scrub from her purse. Keeping those In the bathroom, she switched on the geyser.

Looking at herself in the big wall size mirror, she said, "Wow!" She was obsessed with herself and would never get tired of looking at herself in the mirror and praising and criticising her own beauty at the same time.

***

"Naina, I just sent messages to six people. Three of them will definitely come. And if I get three new tonight, then total six jobs will be done," Manisha said, while chatting over the phone.

Naina was keeping her things back in the wardrobe.

"I can't think of anything else till I collect the money," she said again, a little impatient this time.

"What do you write to them?" Naina asked, while applying body lotion.

Keeping her phone aside, Manisha stretched and yawned. Then she said, "I write all sillybthings that will make them come and meet me here."

"But that's not right. Why are you encouraging them to come here?"

"I need to keep in touch with the customers to make them feel like meeting me time and again," she said as she got up from the bed.

"They will come if they wish. You shouldn't provoke them."

"When customers come here for me, I become the manager's favourite. Then they promote me more. Otherwise, you know how they behave," Manisha said, while selecting a dress for the evening.

"Naina, see this one," holding a royal blue gown, she asked, "How's it for tonight?" Her eyes were twinkling.

"Fabulous," Naina said, "This fish cut shape would look very nice on you."

Manisha smiled. "Whatever you wear, these managers would keep showing the females of their own choice."

"They show them because they are good at repeating customers," Naina said.

"Even I have so much fun with the customers and make them laugh so that they take my name every time. But because of Nisha, the number of my jobs is waning nowadays,"

Manisha said sadly.

"Hmm, once a customer comes to you, he keeps coming to you. That's why you were Peter's favourite. Nowadays, Nisha is taking your place," Naina said, while combing her hair.

"Huh! Don't talk about her," Manisha said. "She takes MD, cocaine and what not. She even gives it to the customers to make them stay here for a longer time.

Look at Rajesh, Zayed and Vijay. They have become totally addicted to MD; they keep coming to her regularly."

Looking at herself in the mirror, Naina said absently, "Hmm, that's bad. You should not encourage someone into drugs."

"Look at Peter, he has all the drug addict customers. Every time he sends a girl inside the room, he says to repeat the job," Manisha said irritatingly.

"This kind of behaviour of the managers' puts so much pressure on all the girls. Who, when gives good service, they promote that girl and all try to give good service to make the customers keep coming to them,"

"Naina, I am going to take shower now. I will lock the door from inside. Will you sit here or

go to the kitchen?" Manisha said. She suddenly realised she was getting late for taking a bath.

" I will go and have lunch. You may lock it from inside," Naina said.

Chapter 6

Simran, Vinita, Monica, Tina and Jiya were having lunch sitting on a wooden bench placed outside the kitchen. Naina sat beside them. There was dal, mixed vegetable curry, rice and goat meat for lunch. Suresh was serving lunch. He gave Naina a plate having dal, rice and vegetable curry.

"Naina, aren't you having meat?" Monica asked. She was a newcomer there.

"No, I have stopped eating non-vegetarian food," Naina said.

"Really?" She was astonished. "When?"

"Five months back."

"But why?" She was inquisitive.

Vinita asked, "Why, Naina? You never told us the reason; we have asked you before but you avoided giving an answer." Then looking at Monica, she said, "Will you believe now if I say, Naina used to eat non-vegetarian food three times a day. Naina and Saloni used to order chicken and other non-vegetarian food every day from the restaurant."

Monica raised her eyebrows and forgot to bring them down. Then she opened her mouth.

"What are you saying? Is it true, Naina?" She asked with utter surprise.

"It is a fact," Naina said. Then looking at Vinita, she said, "I don't tell the reason because I don't want to hurt your feelings. You all eat meat. I can't make you stop eating them, so what is the use of simply telling about me?"

"We can't control our greed or addiction for non-vegetarian food, it is our limitation. I must appreciate your sacrifice of taste. You can tell us the reason," Vinita said. It seemed she realised what sacrifice truly meant.

"Thank you, Vinita. You just told the reason," Naina said. "This is called sacrifice. Sacrifice of mundane sensual desire, which doesn't let me grow in the path of devotion and spirituality.

Killing some living being in order to fulfil my own selfish desire doesn't help me grow spiritually.

"When I was a non-vegetarian, then I was unaware of myself. I didn't know myself. So, I used to eat animals. Now, I know myself so I don't eat any animal now. I stopped eating innocent animals because of my compassion and love for them."

"You said that you know yourself, so you don't eat animals. Do you mean to say animals are not different from you?" Tina enquired.

"Animals too have a soul inside their body. This soul is the part of Lord Krishna. So, the same soul which is in my body, that is there in their body too. We all are God's children. Soul is eternal and will change its costume in next birth. Soul continues its journey.

"But when somebody kills innocent animals, soul leaves the body forcefully. Imagine how much pain and suffering that animal goes through. When those animals are kept within a cage, they wait for their death; they know that death is near and start feeling death before dying, just think what goes on in their mind.

"Animals have emotions and feelings. They get frightened and scared and wait for their turn to be killed. Imagine their helplessness at that very moment when they are going to be killed. So many hormones are secreted and get mixed in their blood and the muscles that we eat.

"The pain and fear their senses go through while they are being killed is negative energy that they are passing while dying. Our body receives energy from the food we eat. Our body receives the energy of pain, violence, negativity, helplessness, anxiety, fear from meat and our nature becomes violent and negative.

"The energy of pain, fears, and violence that we consume through food make us feel painful, afraid and violent in small matters. We can actually stay calm and positive when we consume Satwik food. We all are God's children having the same soul which is there in an animal's body and in our body too, then why to enjoy other's suffering?" Naina asked, looking at them.

"The way you feel for the animals, I don't feel that way," Jiya said.

"That's because the level of consciousness is different between us."

"Though I am eating meat but what you said is correct. It affects us in so many ways. It is an act of violence, which reduces kindness, generosity, and compassion in human nature," Monica said.

"Yes Monica, we are not personally killing the animals but we know that we are eating anvanimal's body, flesh, bones. We are becoming a part of the violence. We see animals be killed in front of our eyes and blood come out from their body. Their body parts are cut in pieces in front of our eyes.

"In the form of meat, we eat pain, fear, negativity, and helplessness. We get energy from the food we eat and we perform action according to our energy. We will not evolve as human beings if we keep eating them. We hear their last painful scream before dying and all these are getting stored in our subconscious mind. Our subconscious mind is the storehouse of all we see, here, watch and do.

"Our nature gets influenced and we also knowingly or unknowingly behave in that manner. We become what we see, so we too become violent. We should love innocent animals. We should care for them. Just for taste of the tongue, we should not kill them. This world is their house too."

"We must sacrifice our violent desire of eating innocent animals to be able to find love and peace within us."

"I will stop meat eating too," Monica said.

"Madam, do you need anything?" Suresh asked all of them.

"Give me a little dal, Suresh," Naina said.

"Give me some curry," Monica said.

"Naina, would you like to taste some pickle?" Tina offered, "Aarti has got mango pickle from her hometown."

"Where is Aarti? When did she come?"

"She came early morning today," Tina said cheerfully, "She had got sweets for all."

"Good to hear that," Naina said as she tasted little pickle.

"It's tasty," she said, " but where is Aarti?"

"She is at her Khar road house. She will take rest for two days. She just came here, gave me the things to give you all and went. She will come from day after tomorrow."

"Oh, okay."

"It is so tough to stop eating meat because of its taste and protein content in it," Vinita said.

Naina took a deep breath. Looking at Vinita affectionately, she said, "When we increase qualities of goodness and raise our vibration, then our intelligence will be able to control our mind and guide us in the right direction. When our awareness is elevated, then we naturally stop eating meat.

"Also, you should think that we cannot create any living being; we can make only toys. How limited is our creativity that we cannot create another living being like us or any other animal.

What is our right to kill them? They are not natural food of human beings.

"And what you are telling about the taste, that taste is our greed, temptations, and addiction which we must control. The greed and addiction are illusions which only appears in our mind. We can control our desire and mind by being determined to do righteous action."

Jiya asked, "Is the job what you are doing now as a prostitute, righteous?"

"No, this job is not righteous. But at present, I am in such a situation that I have to do this.

My mind is not attached with my job and the effect of it. I am doing it as my work, as the source of earning."

Monica said, "Nowadays research says, non-vegetarian food increases chances of cancer and many other diseases. Animals have a lot of mucus and fat, which is not good for our body. Animals definitely have lots of protein in them. Everybody has lots of protein in their flesh. But those proteins are good for their own body. **Antibiotics are used in animals for various reasons. When we consume those animals, it damages our body** from within. Animal eating is one of the main reason of many viral deases.

"Our digestive system is actually not meant for eating meat. While cooking some animal, uou need to use so much of heat, oil and other spices which affects our digestive system. All the non-vegetarian food has a lot of toxins. The quality of the food is Tamasik, so naturally the nature will become Tamasik."

"These animals are produced and slaughtered for eating purposes only," Jiya said.

Naina felt hurt. She looked at Jiya's face for a few seconds. Letting out a deep breath, she said, "Your consciousness is so low that you are only concerned about your own pleasure and likes and dislikes. So, you produce these animals to be killed and be your food. How easily you cook a living being but do not feel any compassion for them. You have plenty of choices for eating vegetarian food but you have a tendency to enjoy other's suffering.

"You are killing these animals because you have killed yourselves much before as human beings, so you are not bothered about their pain. You are selfish; you can do anything and go to any extent for fulfilling your own selfish desire. Where is eternal consciousness bliss? Your mind is covered with the dust of ignorance."

Others kept silent.

Manisha, Saloni, Sofia, Rianka and Sheena came to have lunch. Rianka asked, "Hey, Jiya! Did they make the meat tasty?"

Jiya closed her eyes as if the goat meat was still in her mouth. Relishing the taste once again, she said, "Just awesome!"

Looking at her, Simran said to Naina, "Your words didn't seem to have any impact on her."

Naina said, "It's okay. Some people learn things early and some take time. You also need balance in the earth. Everyone cannot be same."

While washing hands, Simran asked, "Naina, you don't mind if I ask you something?"

"You can ask me."

"You stopped eating non-vegetarian food. You listen to devotional songs and spiritual speeches on YouTube. Then why don't you stop this work? Is this work not sin according to you?"

She smiled at her. "Since my school days, I used to listen to a lot of music and read lots of story books and novels. I am not doing anything suddenly. I am just trying to understand spirituality because I am basically a studious person. I like to read and study.

"This job of prostitution is a sin. My difficult situation had brought me into this profession because I wanted to live, I am clearing my karmic account here. Someday, I will definitely do something else. Till then, I am acquiring knowledge that is an act of merit and virtue. The more we learn about 'Gita' and Lord Krishna, we learn self-knowledge. We receive God's grace and can be free from sins."

"But Naina, don't you regret being in this profession?"

"Suppose, I would have been doing something else, anything else other than prostitution, I wouldn't have much time to listen to such spiritual knowledge because I would have been busy in my day to day-to-day work of family or office. But here, I get a lot of time to learn the divine knowledge, I earn money and I send them at home so I don't have tension of how to run the family.

"I don't have to cook food ; I get it all ready. So, I have a lot of free time here. So, why don't you think of it in this way that I have used my time in the best way possible to learn the truth of life."

"Beautiful, we should try to look for positivity in every situation and make the best use of any situation that we have got in life. We must learn from every situation. Most of us waste our time by regretting about what we do not have in life, and that negativity becomes a part of our nature. We should practice to see what we have in our life; we should choose to stay positive."

Naina nodded her head. She said, "Living in a society, all the time it is not possible to stay positive. Sometimes we may feel stressed, left out, angry, depressed, and sad too. But if we have more Satvik qualities then we can overcome those negative feelings. We can overcome our negative feelings and thoughts by being in the association of spiritually elevated people.

"Our true happiness is in God, love, serving the human and animals, sharing, andvcaring for people and receiving the same as well. We need to enquire from within. The more we know about Lord Krishna, Gita, astrology, and our scriptures. This makes us feel truly joyful and blissful from within."

"You have made the best use of a bad bargain," Monica said.

Chapter 7

"There could be a police raid soon," Raju announced and a ripple of worried murmurs filled the inside hall room.

"Girls, change and go home. Hurry up," Sunil said.

"Everyone, get down from the window, hurry up! Fast," Suresh said as he came running. The females looked at each other, picked up their purses and ran in different directions. There was one window in the kitchen and another window was in the last room at the corner.

Pinky, Kajal, Nisha, Sheena were wearing open short dresses. Few people were wearing heavy saris but at that time, everyone had to save themselves. Some of them gathered near the kitchen window and got down, holding the water pipe. Rest of them gathered in the corner room.

There was a girl named Mansi. She got so scared while getting down that she slipped and fell down from the window. She screamed once. Zarina kept her palm on Mansi's mouth and stopped her from shouting. Zarina helped her to get up and stand on one side.

Just below the window, there was a drain. People used to throw the garbage there because It was a blind lane. So, it was safe for them to hide there for some time because no one would come there. Later, they jumped on the other side of the lane to run away.

Sofia, Saloni, Ishika, and Naina met on the main road. The yellow and white street lights of the evening were shining brightly. Cars and buses were continuously running on both the sides of the roads. They stood at one side of the busy road of Mumbai. Sofia suggested them to go to her rented house at Mira Road and try some new recipes.

Mira Road was quite far from where they stayed but they agreed. Sofia was always enthusiastic about trying new recipes and sharing the food among her friends

She said, "Let's make paneer butter masala and mix pulao tonight."

"Did you have the menu in mind from before? Or you just thought of it?" Saloni asked.

"I was watching a new preparation of paneer on YouTube last week. Today, we have got a chance," she giggled, "So let's do it."

"Cool. We'll buy the ingredients from the market near your house," Ishika said.

"Should we buy the beer and whiskey now on the way?" Naina said.

"That will be better," Saloni said.

***

Sofia had two rooms in that house and a dining hall. The kitchen was spacious. After the food was ready, they were sitting in the dining hall. Sofia was cutting cucumbers and carrots for salad. She loved doing it for herself and for all.

"How is your brother-in-law, Sophia?" Ishika asked.

"What happened to your brother-in-law?" Saloni enquired.

"He had got a severe cerebral attack yesterday. He is in the hospital now." Sofia's smiling face was immediately sad.

"Did you take loan from Lala ji?"

"Veena madam has spoken with Lala ji. I will get the loan by tomorrow. Kunal has some money in his account but they need more. The expenditure in any private hospital is beyond the reach of middle-class people. And in the government hospital, you won't get all kinds of treatment and medicine within your budget," Sofia said as she sighed.

"You are depositing cash in his account that is only enough. You don't need to go and see him personally in Calcutta. You better work here to give back the money soon," Ishika said.

"I am not going to Calcutta now. My daughter is in her final year of studies in school. She will get admission in college next year. I will have to arrange money for her college fees and all," Sofia said.

"Why do you need to do everything? Kunal should do something now," Saloni **asked**.

Sofia had cut the salad. Keeping the plate aside, she said, "Kunal totally depends on my earnings. But I cannot blame him also because my mother-in-law and brother-in-law werevnot well. He was the only person who took care and looked after all of them including my ownvmother, brothers, and sisters.

"My daughter was too difficult to handle and very much attached with her father. Kunal raised her up with proper guidance as much as he could with his little education but high moral values."

"What brought you here? Tell us," Ishika said.

"Saloni knows everything. She will tell you," Sofia said.

Saloni loved talking. She took a large sip of beer and then went on.

***

Those days, Sofia had a family of six people; father-in-law, mother-in-law, brother-in-law, her daughter Diya and husband Kunal. One day, Kunal's factory got closed and he lost his job. That was a real tough time. He did not get any new job anywhere. Sofia was also struggling to get a job somewhere. But with her little education, she could not find any job. She started working as a housemaid in a few houses. Thus, they were surviving somehow.

One day Sofia went to her parents' house. She took her daughter along with her. As she pressed the doorbell, her mother opened the door and got excited seeing Sofia and Diya after a long time.

"Soma," she called Sofia by her nickname. "You came after so many months. I was continuously thinking about you from past few days," she said as she held Sofia's hands in joy. Sofia was feeling overwhelmed. She hugged her mother. After a long time of struggles and hardships, a day came that brought a smile on her face. The warmth of her mother's hug absorbed all her sadness within moments it seemed.

"My little baby, Diya," Mother said, "Come, come inside." She caressed her. They went inside the house. It was a rented and old one. Paints were almost nil on the walls. Sofia and Diya sat on the bed. Mother switched on the fan and told her, "You take some rest, I am getting tea for you."

"It's okay, Maa. I don't need tea now," she said, holding her mother's hands. "You sit here."

"You have become so thin. You look so exhausted. Aren't you taking care of yourself?"

Mother asked worriedly.

"I don't have time for myself nowadays," Sofia said, "Kunal doesn't listen to anything and if I tell him to work, it makes him irritated," she almost cried like a child.

Mother kept her palm on Sofia's head and stroked her hair, consoling that things would be fine someday. Something struck her mother's mind suddenly. Leena came from Mumbai last week. Sofia would be happy to meet her after a long time and would forget her worries for some time, she thought.

"Leena came from Mumbai last week, she was looking for you," Mother said.

"Leena has come. That's great!" Sofia's face was immediately bright. "What is she doing nowadays?" She was suddenly enthusiastic.

"Leena was looking very beautiful. She was wearing very nice clothes."

"Wow, really?" Sofia grinned.

"Yes, I asked her what she is doing in Mumbai. She said she works in a big hotel as a housekeeping staff," Mother said.

Sofia was glad to hear that. Now, she could see some ray of hope. "Maa, it is good news, I can also try to get a job in Mumbai."

"What!" Mother almost screamed. "Job in Mumbai?"

"Yes Maa, she is my childhood friend and very helpful too. She will definitely help me in finding some job where she works."

"But Mumbai is so far. I can't think of you going so far leaving your family behind." Mother was not convinced.

"If I too get a job there, I can help you in Mitali and Jhumki's marriage. I can help you with money to continue Jay's studies, as well as I can look after my family too," Sofia said.

"Leena is not married; she can live anywhere freely but you have your daughter and family,"

Mother said, "You have never lived a single day without them."

"Maa, if I stay here with my daughter, I can raise her up with all my love and care. But being here, what good will I do for her? Kunal is not getting a new job. How will we give good education and nutrition to Diya? She will also remain uneducated, poorpoor, and helpless like me. And later in life, she will work as a housemaid. We don't even have money to save for her marriage. The life I have seen, I don't want my daughter to go through the same," Sofia said, her voice firm.

Mother could not deny what she just said. She told, "You go and meet her. It is not that easy to just go and get a job. Listen to what she says."

"That's true. If Diya has education and nutrition in her luck, if you have money in your luck, Jhumki, Mitali, and Jay have their luck to get help from me for their marriage and studies, if my husband and his family have their luck to get help from me, then I will definitely get a job. So many people's luck is associated with the job which I may get." She smiled.

"True, we all are interconnected and interrelated."

"I should go and meet her now. Let Diya be here with you, Maa," Sofia said.

"Okay but come back soon," Mother said.

"Where is Meetali and Jhumki? I have not seen them since I have come," Sofia enquired.

"They went to learn sewing. Mitali will join a tailoring shop from the next month. She has spoken there. She will get fifteen hundred rupees per month salary."

"Okay Maa, I am going." Sofia left.

***

Leena was looking at a film magazine sitting on a chair at the compound of their house. She was looking very pretty and glamorous. Seeing her childhood friend suddenly in front of her eyes, Leena was so surprised. She embraced her. "I am so happy to see you after so long time!"

Sofia was equally happy. "Leena, look at you, you are looking so beautiful. You have changed so much," Sofia said as she sat on a chair.

After exchanging a few more pleasantries, Leena noticed that even though Sofia was smiling and talking, she was trying hard to hide something.

She asked Sofia, "How are youyou, Soma? We are seeing each other after a very long time. You are looking tired. Is everything alright?"

"No, nothing is okay. But if I start saying all this, you will think I have started my story as soon as I came," Sofia said in a gloomy voice.

"Please don't be so formal. We are childhood friends. You don't need to explain so much,"

Leena said, "Wait, let me make some coffee for you."

"No, it's okay, I don't need coffee now. You sit here," Sofia said.

" Aha, it's not okay to not have coffee with you. We are meeting after so long time, we should celebrate. I have got some cookies from Mumbai; you should try them," Leena said and went inside.

Sofia was sitting quietly and thinking if Leena could help her in finding some job in Mumbai , then she would solve all her house problems. She would continue Diya's school and help her mother for Meetali and Jhumki's marriage. At the moment when her sisters were getting married in Sofia's dream, Leena entered with a big tray in hand as if she was the host of the marriage function welcoming Sofia as their guest. Sofia blushed at her day dreaming.

There were two cups of coffee, cookies, cake, and roasted cashews on a tray. Keeping them on the table, she said, "Please have these first. Then tell me what's going on in your life."

"You have got so much," Sofia said and took a cake. Having a small bite, she said, "Nice soft cake, it just melted in my mouth, chocolate flavour. The cookies look delicious too. You get nice things in Mumbai."

"I have got some more snacks. You take some for Diya before you leave. Wait, I will just get them." Leena went inside again.

Sofia was thinking, if she was to get a job in Mumbai, she could provide good healthy food and clothes to Diya. She would admit her in an English medium school, buy new saris for her mum, mother-in-law and buy new dresses for Jhumki and Meetali. She was in her own dreams. In the middle of her dream, when she was thinking how her daughter would look in a new school uniform, Leena got a packet and gave it to Sofia saying that's for Diya. A sad smile appeared on Sofia's face for a moment. She said, "From past few months, I couldn't give her any good food. I feel so bad." Her eyes filled with tears.

"Please don't cry, tell me what happened." Leena patted Sofia's shoulder.

Wiping her eyes, Sofia said, "I am in serious problem. I need your help very badly. Please help me to find some job. Kunal lost his job almost a year back. He couldn't find any new one."

Leena took a deep breath, after some moments of silence, she said, "The same problem was there at my house too. My brother didn't get any job. All the time, he used to buy lottery tickets in the hope of winning a big amount of money. For buying lottery tickets, he used to ask money from me. The younger brother is driving a car and earning. I helped him in buying the car."

Sofia looked surprised. She said, "You are in Mumbai from last three years, how much do you earn in a month?

"It depends, there is no fixed income. I get commission on the total payment."

"Still, you earn good money. The car that your brother is driving, is that new or old?"

"A new car?" Leena's eyebrows together formed a second bracket on her forehead. She said,

"What are you saying? Where will I get so much money from? That is a second-hand old car."

Sofia said, "You are doing so much for your brothers, they will definitely be with you in the future."

"I don't expect that. I don't know whether they will be with me or not, that is not my worry. I am doing my part, that's all." Leena was cool. Then she asked, "Leave it. You tell me, what is going on in your life?"

"You can guess the situation I am going through after Kunal lost his job. You know how difficult it is to run a big family with little money. Last year, Diya was admitted in a school nearby. Food, school fees, everything is becoming so difficult to arrange. I work in three houses and get so less payment.

"I don't know how many days I will be able to run the expenditure of all of them. My father-in-law remains sick most of the time. Brother-in-law is handicapped. All these things are giving me tension. I want to earn some more money," Sofia said as she let out a breath of frustration.

Leena was listening quietly.

"What job are you doing in Mumbai? My mother said you are working in some hotel. Can't I get a job at your place? I am ready to do any work," Sofia said anxiously.

Leena looked down on the floor while thinking what to say to Sofia about her job. Should she say the truth or should she tell something else?

"What happened? Why aren't you saying anything?" Sofia was eagerly waiting for her reply.

Leena looked at her and said slowly, "If I tell you the truth, you may not like it. But I trust you, we are childhood friends. Whether you like it or not, whether you do the job or not, you will keep it a secret."

"Of course that goes without saying," Sofia assured her friend.

"Then listen, I sleep with different people and get a percentage for each of them. I work as a prostitute."

"What!" Sofia screamed so loud as if someone had slapped her face. She couldn't speak for some time. After some time, she mumbled, "I mean, how this is possible. This is unbelievable! I can't even imagine it in my wildest dream." Sofia's face looked even gloomier. All her dreams were shattered.

"This is my truth. You have to believe it," Leena said.

"Why? No other job was available other than this?" It seemed Sofia would cry again. She had started seeing beautiful dreams of a healthy normal life. But is this a way to get a normal healthy life?

Leena asked her, "Did you get any other job? You must have tried a lot."

Sofia swallowed the lump in her throat. Her eyes were welling, tear drops ran down her cheeks.

"I didn't have much choice," Leena said. Her eyes got watery too. Sofia didn't speak. Silence prevailed between the two.

After some time, Sofia broke the silence. "How difficult it is to sleep with so many different people for money?"

"Can you tell me something that is easy in life? You need to pay a price for everything,"

Leena said in a firm voice. "Hunger and necessity of my life have a bigger say than my personal feelings. When I sleep with a customer, I don't think about my body, feelings or anything like that, whatever I am doing I am doing it for me to live and to feed my family. Smile on their faces makes me feel good."

Sofia was thinking. She was in a dilemma. She asked, "Isn't it a shortcut to earn money?"

"People who say this, will they take care of the needs of me and my family? Whatever you do, people will always have their own views. But ultimately, it's you who has to make a choice for living. Hardly people help until they have some personal selfish motive behind helping you. Moreover, it is not a shortcut, it is very difficult. If you do, you will understand. It is painful," Leena said.

Sofia was looking at her friend, thinking how casually she was saying all this. She was not convinced yet for any such work. She kept quiet.

After sometime Leena said, "Who wants such shortcut willingly, Soma? If you have so many people in the family to look after, then you don't have much choice. You know my family situation very well. I know, I am earning in a wrong way but this is the only available way to save myself and my family.

"I am going through different problems but my mother, my brothers, they are happy. If you want, I can take you there, you can look after your family too. If you don't want, don't go. I will be going in the next week."

Sofia thought she had to take some decision soon, otherwise her problems of her house would never be solved. She thought her friend was right to say that hunger and necessities have a bigger say in life than anything else. She made up her mind.

"It is a difficult decision but I think I will go with you there. My financial condition is so critical that somehow, I need a solution."

"Don't worry. I am there with you," Leena assured her.

"When will you be going in the next week there? I don't have any money for buying tickets," Sofia said.

"I will buy your tickets and few clothes too," Leena said, "You need some good clothes there. We can go to the market together today if you want. Later, you can give back the money when you earn."

Sofia was worried. She was not thinking about clothes at that moment. "But, what will I say at my home, what do I do in Mumbai?" She said.

"I said I work in a hotel as a housekeeping staff," Leena said, "I sometimes help in other works too, so I get tips from the boarders. Everybody knows people earn good money in Mumbai. You can say that too." She made tough things easier for Sofia.

"Okay. I will talk at home today; you can book my tickets too. But I don't want to go for shopping now. I have other things going on in my mind."

"That's fine, as you say," Leena said as she held Sofia's hands while consoling and telling her to keep cool as these situations come and go, as part of life. Sofia was slowly becoming calm.

"Thank you for saving my family." Sofia finally expressed her gratitude towards Leena.

Someone had showed some way to earn money to live a better life than what she was living from last one year, Sofia thought.

"Whether am I saving your life or pushing you towards more darkness, that I am not sure. But this is what I could do, so I did. But you need to change your name there," Leena said in a monotone.

Sofia was thinking something deep within her mind. Her eyes were lost somewhere trying to see something far away that was not visible though. She murmured, "I remember when I was very young, one evening I happened to cross a road in the city. Ladies were standing there on the road for getting customers. Looking at them, I was astonished.

"I thought how someone sleeps with so many different people! What kind of women are they! Even the thought of sleeping with a person without love and marriage was a nightmare for me. I was staring at them with a mixed feeling of repulsiveness, inquisitiveness and sympathy. It's difficult for me to explain."

Leena could understand how her friend was feeling then. She kept quiet.

"You know, I just stopped for some moments on that road just to see them because it was one of the most difficult things what they were doing," Sofia said. "That day I didn't know, I will be one of them someday." Sofia let out a deep breath.

***

Sofia came home with a lot of tension and thoughts. Though she agreed to work as a prostitute but mentally, she was not prepared at all. She was quiet at home than she normally used to be. Kunal noticed something was wrong. He asked, "What happened to you, Soma?

Since you came back from your parents' house, you are quiet!"

It was tough for her to lie. But then she gathered all her strength together to control her overflowing emotions within. "I have got a job in a hotel in Mumbai. My childhood friend Leena also works there. She earns good money. If I go, I will also earn good money. So, I was thinking what to do." She held her emotions to lie in a flat tone.

"Do whatever you wish." Kunal shrugged his shoulders.

"I am worried about Diya's school fees. You are not earning anything. How will I manage alone with the increasing expenses?" Sofia said.

"What work will I do? I am trying to get a job but not getting any," Kunal said.

"You say this every time."

"Then stop asking me."

"Fine, I will go to Mumbai with Leena."

"Do whatever you want."

"If I go, then who will look after Diya?

"If you want, you can go to Mumbai. My mother will take care of Diya."

"Your mother doesn't keep well most of the time. How would she look after Diya? I will not go to Mumbai if you do some work here. You can do any work," Sofia begged.

Kunal was irritated. "There is no job in the market. I have not completed school. With my little education, I was working in the factory, where will I work now?"

"The same excuse again and again."

"Whether you look after our family or not, doesn't matter. You can go to your parents' house. It is up to you," he almost screamed.

"What you people will eat if I leave this house?" Sofia was annoyed. "Can't you even work in some shop?"

"Am I telling you to take care of us? Go wherever you want to go. Otherwise, be here but don't tell me what to do."

Sofia kept quiet; she knew after losing his job, Kunal had become impatient. He couldn't keep his calm. Any small thing spoken could initiate a fight. She composed herself.

***

Sofia and Leena were sitting opposite to each other on the window seats of a train, which would take them to Mumbai. Kunal brought Diya with him to the railway station. They were standing on the platform. The train was about to leave. Diya started crying, "Maa, where are you going? Maa?"

"I am going for work, Diya."

"How far are you going? How far does this train go?"

Diya wanted to come out from her father's arms, she wanted to touch her mother. Kunal went near the window of the train. Sofia touched her daughter and said, "Diya, you will go to school now, papa will get dolls and games for you and lots of chocolates. Be with your grandmother, be good."

Diya put her hand over her father's shoulder tightly, she was going on crying, asking her father, "Papa, will you also leave me and go like Maa is going?"

Kunal took her in his arms, held her tightly and said, "Don't cry Diya, I will never leave you and go, your mother will come back soon."

The train took its speed, slowly Kunal and Diya went out of sight. Sofia could not stop herself from crying. She covered her eyes with her palms and broke out into tears. Her whole body was shivering. Leena got up from her seat and embraced her.

In Mumbai, Soma's new name was Sofia. She got a new name and a new life all together which identity was true in her life, Soma-wife of Kunal, mother of Diya, daughter of her parents, sister of Jhumki, Mitali and Jay or Sophia, a prostitute for the customers?

***

"She is a human being, that's her main identity above anything else," Ishika said as Saloni finished telling the life story of Sofia.

"True," Saloni said.

"Sofia is so concerned about all the people of her family. Her husband doesn't work but takes out cash from her account every month," Ishika said.

"That is the reason her husband does not work at all. If he gets everything ready at home, why will he work? Thus, these men get spoilt with our money. We are also bound to send money home because we came here to earn for them, later they don't earn. And even if they earn, they and their family will save their own money like a miser and spend our money lavishly," Saloni said.

Naina didn't want to comment in anyone's personal matter. She didn't want to know either but when you are with a group of people, staying with them day and night, you can't avoid things entering into your ears. She kept quiet.

After some time, they changed the topic and were talking about something else. Naina came out and stood in the balcony with her glass filled with whisky. As the night was becoming darker, the stars and the moon seemed to shine brighter. Looking at the night sky, she got lost somewhere until Saloni came there and snapped her fingers in front of her eyes.

"Naina, where are you?" Saloni said.

Naina got back into the present. "I was watching the moon. Look, it's beautiful. Isn't it?"

Saloni patted her shoulder. "Come, let's eat," she said.

Chapter 8

"Hey, Naina! Where are you?" Meghna snapped her fingers in front of her eyes. Meghna, who was looking absolutely stunning in a white salwar kameez and fuchsia dupatta along with her trademark style large oxidised dazzling earrings, just came from Char bungalow, where she lived in a chawl at MHADA, sharing the room with Maahi. Maahi used to work at another flat near Grant Road.

"Oh hi! How are you?" Naina said, surprised.

"You are always lost somewhere, Naina. What's the matter with you?" Meghna said.

"Nothing serious, I was thinking about something that I just read in Google," Naina said.

"Don't think all the time. Talk with us sometimes," Meghna said, "When will you do your make-up?"

Naina smiled as she opened her purse to take out kajal and eyeliner. After lunch, Naina was sitting in the inside hall. Sarah, Muskan, Aarohi and Nafisa were also there. Meghna took out a chilled bottle of water from the refrigerator. After drinking some water, she kept the bottle on a shelf. Sitting on a bench she asked, looking at them, "So, how is everything here?"

Naina smiled at her and said, "Just fine. How are uncle and aunty? Did you show them all the

good places in Mumbai?"

"I just went to the Elephanta Caves one day with maa and baba. It was tiring," Meghna said,

"Now I've talked with a travel agent who will arrange for their Mumbai trip."

"That's good. They can travel and go wherever they want without bothering you. And you can come at work," Nafisa said.

Meghna's parents from West Bengal had come last week. They would stay the whole month here. Meghna was accompanying them. She came at work after a week. Meghna smiled at Nafisa. "Do you remember I used to take regular medicine to stop my periods for months?"

Meghna said, looking at her.

"Yes, I do. Why, what happened?" Nafisa was inquisitive.

"In the last month, I stopped taking medicine and guess what?" She asked, widening her eyes.

"What?" Nafisa and Aarohi said in unison.

"My period was not starting," Meghna said.

"That can be a serious health issue," Naina said.

"It already is serious, Naina," Meghna said. "I went to a doctor. After all the medical tests,

He said to me to undergo go for a surgery."

"Is it that serious?"

"Yes, it is," Meghna said and then she looked at Nafisa and told her, "You too stop periods for months, don't do it anymore."

"I can't take five holidays in a month. You know there are six people in the family and the only earning member is me," Nafisa said.

"Jeni, Simran, Kajal, Manisha, Sarah and Jiya also take medicine to stop periods for many months," Muskan said.

Everybody fell silent.

"All madams," Suhas broke the silence, "Please go to that side of the hall, Sunil ji is calling."

Walking along the corridor, they reached the lounge outside. Three people aged around thirty were sitting on the sofa. Seeing them coming, Sunil switched on the lights. The hall was full with women. Customers were looking at them silently. Sunil introduced them to the customers.

"From the left side sir, Rani, Sarah, Nafisa, Sheena, Priya, Aarohi, Muskan, Sofia, Naina, Meghna, Ishika, Monica, Nikita, Jiya, Tina, Kajal, and Jeni."

"Now say, sir," Sunil said.

"No more girls are there?" One of them asked.

"There are few others but they are busy now."

One of the customers was looking at Naina from the start when they entered. Then he looked

at the other women. Again, his eyes were on Naina. Naina also noticed that and smiled at him as usual. He said, "Black top, blue jeans."

"Naina, go inside," Sunil said.

Naina smiled at the customer once again and came back where she was sitting before. After some time, Babloo told her, "Madam, go to room number four for two hours. I am coming with the room service."

Naina knocked on the door and stepped inside.

"Hi!"

"Hi! I am Ishan," he said as he came forward and shook hands with her.

Naina smiled and kept her purse and mobile on the side table. Both sat on the bed.

"Would you like to try some joints?" Ishan asked.

"No, thanks!" Naina said, smiling. "I don't like smoking joints but I like whiskey."

"Oh, okay cool. How many pegs will be good for you?"

"Two for now."

Naina displayed her best smile.

Babloo came in with the room service. "Do you need anything, sir?' He asked, keeping the things on the side table.

"Two pegs of Antiquity Blue, cold drinks and wafers."

"Sir, room service and money for the drinks, please," Babloo said.

"Can't you take it later? I may extend time if I wish," Ishan said.

"No, sir. I have to go downstairs in the main road to get the drinks, so you please pay now."

Ishan shrugged his shoulders. "Okay, as you wish!" He took out his purse and paid. Babloo went off.

"Naina, I am going to the washroom. You may start to drink. You don't need to wait for me.

Anyways, I will be smoking joints. You enjoy your drinks," Ishan said.

"Thank you, Ishan."

He smiled. "Pleasure is mine."

***

After some time, Babloo came inside to serve drinks and wafers. He kept them on the side table and went off. She locked the door. By the time Ishan came out from the washroom, Naina had already finished the first peg and started the second.

Sitting on the bed, he said, "Now I am feeling fresh, all day it was so tiring at the site. So, what were you thinking?"

Naina smiled as she kept her glass aside. "I was thinking about the life of a prostitute," she said.

Ishan was taken aback. "Like?" He wanted to know.

"Tell me one thing honestly, don't you think because we are outside the society, women are safe inside the society? That doesn't mean I am supporting the act of prostitution. When I think of the present situation of our society and the mentality of many men towards women, I think, had we not been there, it would have been difficult for other women to walk and work safely on the road and at their workplace because men don't sacrifice their sexual desire," Naina said.

"To some extent, you are right. Even I find it difficult to control sexual desire," Ishan said.

"You know I have a friend who imagines his cousin sister while having sex and takes her name. But he can't do this with his wife. He comes in brothels."

"Even I have met few customers like that," Naina said.

Ishan had kept a few marijuana cigarettes in a cigarette packet. He took one of that and lit it up. He inhaled a big puff and held the smoke inside for some time. Then he released the smoke through his mouth and nose, making the whole room smoky.

Naina asked him, "Would you mind if I switch off the air conditioner for some time and switch on the exhaust fan?"

He said, "Do whatever you want. You keep the room fresh and pollute the nature," and he was smiling.

"You are polluting your lungs and the environment, making me a passive smoker. When will you sacrifice your desire for addiction?"

"Yeah, smoking is bad," he said casually. "Forget about me, why don't you smoke?"

"I smoked hash and grass before. But I didn't like it. It gave me a heavy head. So, I don't smoke anymore," Naina said.

"Okay."

"But I used to smoke cigarettes a lot, twenty to twenty twenty-five cigarettes a day. Later I stopped smoking. But again I started to smoke cigarettes. It happened many times working in this profession, smoking and quitting ciggerates again and again..."

"It's difficult for me to stop **smoking grass**. I am smoking joints from my college days. I am habituated with it. This is normal for me. I don't feel anything of that sort what you feel," Ishan said.

"Are you smoking joints from your college days? Did you live in a boy's hostel?" Naina asked.

"Yes, we had the ultimate fun and freedom of our life during our college days. Those were the golden days of my life, I still cherish," Ishan said.

"We all cherish our college days. What all did you do in college?' Naina asked.

"You know Naina, I was from a very restricted family background. My father was a very disciplined person. I was not allowed to do something I wanted. I had spent my days at home like I was being punished. Later when I was admitted in the college, I got the taste of freedom for the first time in life. I learnt to drink alcohol. Watching porn videos were our favourite pass time. There we started smoking grass."

"I doubt whether to call it freedom or a knot that has tied you for the whole life."

"The knot was at my house before I joined my college. When we first went to college, then we knew what freedom was. Enjoying alcohol, smoking weed, girlfriend, and pornography, having unlimited chats with friends, sleeping at late night and getting up late. Those were heavenly days. Now see, office, home, and family. No freedom and no fun."

"What you think is freedom is actually preventing you from being free. What you think is freedom has tied you with a knot for the rest of your life, next life and many more lives to come," Naina said.

"Why are you saying this?" Ishan said.

"Let me explain. The habits you developed in college and **college hostel** are addiction, pornography, laziness and gossiping, right?"

"Yes."

"You are still continuing the same habits. You watch pornography. You smoke joints, drink alcohol and meet a lady to satisfy your lust. When you are bored in your sex life within marriage, you immediately look for an easy solution like going for paid sex. Is this what you call freedom?

"Your happiness is getting controlled by the outer factors. Your happiness is dependent on addiction, pornography or having physical pleasure outside the marriage. If you don't get grass in time, you start feeling irritated. The vulgarity shown in pornography excites you negatively. You watch pornography and think of meeting a call girl or you masturbate. Your mind got restricted within all the negative habits you developed.

"And see, you are still continuing the same habits all your life. These habits made you narrow minded to think that only pornography and prostitutes can give you pleasure in sex. But these are superficial negative feelings that encourage you more to indulge in negative things of life. Thus, you go away from true feelings of love and peace.

"You think watching pornography gives you pleasure! Just sit quietly, use your intelligence and analyse how you felt every time you watched pornography. How long did it keep you happy and in what sense? Did you get peace? Or watching pornography regularly made your mind so lustful that any woman you meet, you feel sexually attracted.

"You look at other woman and you think about their nude body. Pornography excites you to watch other people's body. These are very natural thoughts which come into your mind when you watch pornography regularly. You unknowingly lose respect for women.

"You think, it only affects you when you are watching pornography? No, that's not true. It remains in your subconscious mind. It fills your mind with all the lustful thoughts. Though you think that you have suppressed the lustful thoughts but no, it's just the opposite. Lust conquers your mind.

"You are guided by the lust and all your decisions are taken being guided by lust when you watch pornography regularly. And to fulfil your lusty desire, you finally come to a brothel to ejaculate or you masturbate and you lose your vital energy. The lusty expressions which are being shown in the pornography are creating desires within your senses.

"The expression of enjoying sex and orgasm what are being shown in the film is mostly false, just like it happens here in this brothel. You meet ladies, they express themselves just to attract your mind, to make you feel good and take you to cloud nine. It's just their job to do that. They would do that irrespective of how sad they are feeling from within because that is what they get paid for.

"They are earning money and you are losing your vitality. You only think yourself; a lady in a brothel meets so many people every day, how is it possible to have feelings for all? Think logically. Your thoughts have kept you restricted and limited within your own boundary. Your low consciousness didn't let you live for a higher purpose."

Ishan kept quiet. He was thinking. After some time, he said, "These are the things that give pleasure to mind."

"What you think is pleasure, are actually illusionary negative attractions appearing in mind. You remain within the boundary of illusion. You keep running around the knot you have tied your mind with. You can't see beyond when you keep yourself limited within your own boundary.

"You tell me, how long do you enjoy watching pornography or smoking a joint or having sex? You enjoy it for that much time which is allowed to you by your senses. You smoke till you reach a particular state of mind. You enjoy sex until you ejaculate. You enjoy pornography till you masturbate.

"You satisfy your senses and again after some time, your senses tickle you for the same momentary pleasure. Again, you run behind it. Thus, it keeps you running on your shoes. You speak lies, you cheat your wife, you manipulate people, waste your time and money to fulfil these sensual desires. You surround yourself with negative energy, you respond easily with the negative energy.

"Tell me, don't you feel restless, frustrated, depressed, guilty, tensed, worried or violent for small issues or petty reasons? You can analyse your thoughts and nature. And then tell me how the habits of smoking joints and watching pornography made you free or gave you freedom when you are actually dependant on them?"

Ishan had no answer for this. He looked spellbound. He let out a deep breath and got immersed in deep thought. Naina took her cell phone from the side table. She looked into it absently while going through the notifications on the screen of her phone.

Chapter 9

"What, according to you, will make me free? What is freedom?" Ishan asked after a good long break.

Naina kept her phone aside. She looked at Ishan and smiled. "You are a soul, a part of Brahman or the supreme soul and the soul is free. We create bondage of karma for the soul by attaching ourselves with Maya. So, the soul remains trapped within Maya until it pays back the karma associated with it. When you know yourself, that knowledge makes you free from illusionary ties of Maya," she said.

"What do you mean by illusionary ties of Maya?" Ishan's next question came after a little pause.

Naina took a deep breath before explaining. "Illusion is the always changing unreality. Illusion is the reflection of energy on matter. Our intelligence reflects the existing consciousness on the screen of our mind. So, we see and experience illusion and keep moving within Maya.

"I will give you an example of illusion. Suppose you were walking in a desert from a long time. You got tired and wanted to have some water but there was no water anywhere. You continued to walk. After some time, you saw a lake full of water was shining brightly just a little away. There were few date trees around the lake and the reflection of the trees in the water of the lake was looking very beautiful.

"You felt so good within and went almost running to drink water from that lake. The faster you were walking to reach the lake, the faster the lake was moving away from you. Thus, you walked a long way but you didn't find any lake. Ultimately you understood, there was no lake at all, everything was just a reflection of energy on matter.

"Sun light was being reflected on the sand and creating the image of lake. This reflection is called Maya. Brahman, the supreme consciousness gets reflected within matter so we are within the Maya. We all have watched three dimensional movies. There we see things appear in front of our eyes at such a close distance that we could touch them.

"But in reality, we know , there was nothing like that to touch. It was appearing because of the reflection of light. Maya is the physical appearance of energy. This appearance is created by the reflection of energy."

"Maya is physical and is subjected to change."

"Yes because the energy is constantly changing its form and so the Maya will."

"But the existing consciousness is eternal."

"Yes. All our actions are performed within the realm of Maya. And we think the world of Maya is our reality. We are involving ourselves more into Maya when our mind is attached In addiction, prostitution, gambling, etc. These things keep us in illusion and we keep revolving around these things. The more we indulge in all these things, more Rajasik and Tamasik qualities are developed within us. Thus, we can never come out from the clutches of Maya."

Ishan said, "The bonding and attachment between people are also Maya."

"We live in the world of Maya or illusion. Any attachment that we have with people or the things and any emotional bonding are also Maya. Emotions are the energy of how we feel. And Maya is the reflected energy that we have and that we exchange.

"When we have this knowledge, then we are aware about the truth, then we observe our life journey and remain less affected by the outer influences. Because then we know that only our qualities are working through this body mind structure according to our higher or lower consciousness."

"It is easy to explain but it is not easy to control the sexual desire and addiction," Ishan said.

"True, it is not easy to control the sexual desire and addiction because we don't try sincerely to control. We follow our instinct and fulfil our desire. If we are hungry, we eat food. So, when you have the urge to have sex, you find an easy solution like going for paid sex.

"You should take such decision based on the priority and necessity of human life. Is it really necessary to have illicit sex without which you feel difficult to survive? Then what is the difference between an animal and a human?" Naina said.

"Human beings are the most intelligent living beings on earth. Animals are not," Ishan said.

"Are human beings making the proper use of their intelligence? Human beings are using their power to get control over others but not over themselves. Human have well developed Brain mechanisms for the intelligence to work through it and reflect higher consciousness on the mind. So, we can enquire about God.

"But the brain and body mechanism of animals are not that developed in them, so their intelligence can't project higher thoughts in their mind. So, they can't enquire about God. The mind, identity and intelligence are present within them as the subtle body from their previous birth along with the past life culture but they can't function due to less developed brain mechanisms," Naina said.

"Mostly the vulgar sexual thoughts come within mind when people feel lonely and seek pleasure, then they tend to see pornography," Ishan said.

"Loneliness is a state of mind when lusty desires are being nurtured. You can overcome loneliness by engaging your mind into acquiring higher knowledge.

Knowledge will make you free from illusionary bondage. You can overcome your lust by living for greater purpose. You can overcome lust by establishing love within your mind.

"You must associate with spiritual people for guidance. Your association is the most important in life to upgrade or degrade yourself. Pornography excites you to masturbate and thus, you lose the most important vital fluid of your body. Thus, the feeling of love goes away and negativity increases in your mind.

"It is so important to retain the semen, which helps in developing brain cells too. But you lose your semen for no good reason and how it is affecting your love relationship with your wife, You can see. from young age, you grew up watching pornography, there you see your darkest negative desires taking place in front of your eyes, so you get easily attracted towards pornography.

"Where is any feeling of love there? It is all about lust. You lose your positivity when you come in the grip of lust. The more you become habituated to see pornography, more you indulge in lust. You lose your love connection with your wife. You think your wife as a caretaker of you, your children, and your home.

"You come here and satisfy your sexual desire in a brothel as you see them in pornography. So, what is the outcome? You are neglecting true love and positivity and inviting falsehood and negativity in life."

Ishan kept quiet.

Naina asked, "Do you feel guilty after having sex here?"

"Naina, I never felt guilty about sleeping with other woman." He took a little pause. Then he said, "I married the person I loved. After marriage, few years were good. Later, the sexual attraction was totally gone. Then I started coming here. I have reason to come to a brothel.

My wife is not interested in physical relations but I have physical urges. I came here because I needed physical release. So, I never felt guilty."

"Sexual attraction was totally gone because you must have indulged too much in sexual activities. You should have limited your sexual activities to hold semen. You married the person you loved. But more than love, it was desire and attraction. Love is faith in each other and love is being within each other. Love is the sacrifice that you do for each other.

"If you would have loved your wife truly, you wouldn't have come here to fulfil your physical need. You would have tried to understand her, why is she reluctant? Why the warmth in relation is no more, you both should have discussed that and made your relation better than before. You both may not enjoy physical pleasure any more, still you will not be able to hurt her feelings by having illicit sex with someone else in love.

"So, it was not love. That is the reason you chose an easy option. You fulfilled your sexual desire outside. Now, the gap between you both became huge. Your relation was based on physical attraction and other superficial things, which have lost value with time. So, you both don't feel attracted towards each other anymore. You are dependent on each other, so you are together."

Ishan kept quiet.

Naina asked him, "How many women have you slept with, here?"

Ishan was thinking, "How many? I come once or twice every month. So, you can guess.__" He stopped midway.

Naina took a deep breath. "How is your wife?" Naina asked.

Ishan took a deep breath. He said, "She, I guess, has all her feelings attached with my monthly salary. She cares not for me but my money. It's her hard-earned money that she lavishly spends at online shopping and parties. She doesn't cook at home. If the maid doesn't come, she orders food online.

"There's nothing homely at my home. At times, I wonder thinking maybe I am living at a hotel. We are together in a house but miles apart from each other. It's our son who keeps us connected. Love, marriage all these are like a mirage, you run after them for happiness and it runs away from you."

"Do you mean this is easy money and it's hard earned in the case of that of a housewife?"

"No, I didn't mean that."

"Good, actually you can't judge someone superficially because you don't know what she is going through in her personal life."

"Hmm, I'll have to take some decision now regarding things that I want to go through." Ishan smiled.

"You can be happy in marriage when you both are spiritually aware, live for higher purpose, are self-content and have total faith in each other. Insecurities and loads of expectations from each other ruin a relationship. When husband and wife both are aware that they are soul, part of Lord Krishna, then you know the absolute truth of life.

"Husband and wife both should do spiritual practices together. When we have spiritual knowledge, we don't get trapped in materialistic desires. When we have self-knowledge,

then we understand our situation and can choose to respond accordingly. You slept with so many women but never got peace in mind, you are always running in search of happiness and engaging yourself in wrong activities.

"Instead, search for higher truth and values in life. Enquire about our scriptures and God.

Ultimately that enquiry will give you happiness and peace. It will raise your vibrations and connect you with the higher realm."

"You are telling husband and wife should practice spirituality together, is that possible?"

"It is possible when you both are associated with spiritual people, then you both develop God consciousness and are guided in the right path. Look, it's not possible for most of us to go in the forest or mountain for practising spirituality. We can be in the society and live for greater purpose and be happy in life."

"What is the purpose of our life?"

"The purpose of our life is to gain self knowledge and be liberated from ignorance. This is called Moksha or 'Jivan Mukti'.."

"Is it possible to attain Moksha in this life?"

"We have to start with Karma Yoga; means performing selfless action as duty without being attached to its result. Then devotion for God can be felt within. Until you understand karma, it is not possible to remove ignorance by the devotion only. True devotion can be felt within when action is done as a devotional service for the Lord.

"You may read the scriptures and then you can meditate to seek within for knowledge. Finally, knowledge removes ignorance. Sometimes, blind devotion without right knowledge makes you selfish."

Naina had to stop as she heard a knock on the door.

"Madam, time-up." It was Suresh knocking on the door from outside.

"Two hours over? I didn't realise," Ishan said, surprised.

"So, how will you live your life now?"

"After all these discussions, I want to bring positive changes in my life. It was nice talking to you. I shall leave now."

"Sure, take care," Naina said.

Chapter 10

Sheena and Vinita were putting streamers, while Aarohi, Kajal and Manisha were sticking balloons on the walls. Sofia played some music on the music player. A triple layered dark chocolate cake was kept on the centre table. Monica, Tina, Ishika, Nafisa and Naina were sitting and watching them decorate the hall. It was Tania's birthday.

Veena, adorably called as Madam by all the people of that brothel, was supposed to look After the overall management. She came to see how the girls were decorating the lounge. During Diwali and New Year, they used to decorate the lounge and corridors with lights and flowers.

"Did you get the sweets from the shop?" Veena asked, looking at Manisha.

"Yes, Madam." Manisha instantly nodded her head.

"Where is the birthday girl?" Veena said.

"Madam, she is getting ready specially. Vicky will come," Manisha said and gave a naughty smile.

"What time is he coming?" Veena saw the time in her wrist watch.

"Around six pm just within half an hour," Manisha said.

Looking at the corridor, Manisha saw Tania was walking towards the lounge. She wore a gorgeous peach colour lacy gown. She was a natural beauty and never did much make up. She would just make her eyes dark with kohl pencil and apply some red or pink lipstick.

Manisha said, "Madam, we were talking about Vicky and Tania appeared."

"You are looking very beautiful. Happy birthday to you," Veena wished her.

"Thank you, Madam," Tania said. Her face was glowing with happiness.

Aarohi, Sheena, Naina, Sofia, and others also came and wished her for her birthday.

Vinita and Manisha had made this plan of celebrating her birthday. They were close friends of Tania and Vicky. They wanted to celebrate not only her birthday but also the togetherness of Tania and Vicky.

"Did Vicky present you this gown?" Veena asked.

"Yes." Holding the edges of the gown, she turned around, showing its back styling. "This is my birthday special. How is it?"

"Beautiful," Veena said.

Tania was a very nice girl, always with a smile on her face. She used to talk very gently with everyone there. Six months back, Vicky met Tania for the first time. After one meeting, they got attracted towards each other. Vicky made a point to come and meet Tania at least once a month. Tania used to meet him outside on all Sundays.

Three months back from now, Veena had asked her, "You both are into a relation now but how serious is this? You know how guys are; they only exploit your body and service. They will talk to you so sweetly and make you feel on top just to use your body and money. I have seen this all my life."

"Madam, Vicky is not like that. He is a true and honest person," Tania said, "And why do you think that only men use women's body and money? A woman also enjoys when she is in a relationship with her man. She loves him, so she gives her money to him for growing together. They both like to be with each other when they are in a relationship.

"Doesn't a woman enjoy physical pleasure with her man? You should come out from such mentality of blaming men for anything and everything. Problems start when we cannot accept each other's faults and shortcomings. Relationship is about acceptance, understanding, faith in each other and growing together."

"If he loves you then ask him to take you from here and marry," Veena said.

"Madam, I had asked him, he will settle things at home first, then we can marry. " Tania said. Veena was worried. "Is he taking divorce from his wife because of you?" She asked.

Tania assured her, "No Madam, it's not like that. He is not taking any divorce. His wife and he are together but they are very different from each other. Their marriage was arranged based on some compromises."

"Oh, okay," Veena said, "But why does he let you work here? Why doesn't he keep you in a separate rented room? Then you don't need to work here anymore. Don't you think a man who loves a girl will take care of her?"

"Madam, please think; if I stop working suddenly, who will look after my family? They are financially dependent on me. My younger sister has just finished her studies. Now she is looking for a job. My brother left his studies. He learnt mobile repairing and just started working at a shop."

"Hmm, you need to give them some time to settle."

"I already told my sister to look for job as soon as possible because I may have to leave my dance bar job soon."

"You told your family that you work in a dance bar?"

"Yes Madam, I told them that I work in a dance bar."

"But an educated graduate girl like you, how did you come in this profession?"

"I never understood my job, neither did I like it. There were financial problems at home."

"Do you like this job of prostitution? Is it better than your previous job?"

"No Madam, I don't like my present job too. But the money I get satisfies all the needs of me and my family. So, I do this."

"But why don't you take the money from Vicky and give to your family?"

"Vicky has his family responsibilities. Also, I don't want to take this money from him. I took my family responsibilities, Vicky was nowhere involved. I cannot ask money from him, later he may help if he feels; if he loves me, he will definitely love my family."

"It is really nice that you both will get married soon. I am really happy for you."

"Thank you, Madam. Vicky told me that he will get me admitted in an Interior Designing Institute after our marriage. I will live my life again, shall help my family too," Tania said.

"Fantastic, you can start your life afresh." Madam was satisfied with her explanation. This conversation took place almost three months back. That day onwards, whenever Vicky came to meet Tania, Veena talked with him very nicely as she believed this person would make his family with Tania. Vicky too mixed up with them like a friend. He used to get sweets, samosa or vada pav for all of them sometimes.

***

"Hello, beautiful," Vicky entered with a flower bouquet in his hand. Giving it to Tania, he wished her first and then greeted everyone seated there.

"How are you, Vicky?" Sofia, Aarohi, and Manisha said in unison. Kajal pinched his arms.

"Hey, Kajal!" He hi-fived with her. Sunil and Sanjay came upstairs and joined them in the celebration. Sheena got a knife to cut the cake. One beautiful candle was placed there on the cake. They wished Tania. She blew the candle and they clapped for her.

She cut the cake and put one small portion in Vicky's mouth. He broke little from that and fed Tania. Kajal took the cake tray to cut the cake in pieces. Aarohi and Manisha served **some** snacks, a cake, and cold drinks to all the people sitting there. Everything was going smooth.

They were chewing snacks or sipping at cold drinks in a relaxed mood until Raju dispelled the gathering by saying, "Madams, you all change and go to your houses. Go slow.

Don't rush in a hurry."

They got up immediately and went to the rooms to change their heavy clothes and wear something simple and light. Inside their workplace, they used to wear flashy, bright coloured, sequined and stone beaded dresses, which were not comfortable for walking on the streets. So, they used to wear jeans and T-shirt or kurti while going out.

Naina's room was locked from inside. She banged on the door of her room. "Who is inside? Please come out soon. We have to leave this place right now."

Immediately someone opened the door. There was Simran inside with a customer.

"Nobody knocked here." Simran was taken aback.

The customer jumped out of the bed and started getting ready. Simran quickly put on her jeans and top, which used to be in her purse all the time. Customer was trembling in fear.

He asked, "How to get down from here?" It was on the first floor.

Naina couldn't control laughing. "You can go from the front, no problem," she said.

He went almost running. Looking at him, now Simran started laughing. Naina quickly changed her dress and came out of the room. Simran asked her, "Naina, where will you go?

At the guest house?"

She said, "Yes, where else?"

Most of the females having family stayed in rented houses. They came at work at around four pm in the evening and went back to their home in the morning after four am. Few females including Naina stayed in the brothel.

Simran said, "You come with me. I will call up Sahil and tell him to make some special dish tonight for us."

Chapter 11

Simran and Sahil used to live at Andheri with two children. Guddu was Sahil's son from his first wife, who used to live with her parents in her village. Later, Sahil and Simran got married and came to Mumbai. Then Tinni was born to them. There was an old lady, a distant relative of Simran, who looked after the children at home.

Sahil didn't work anywhere. He used to stay at home and make new innovative plans for setting up a fast fast-food joint. Simran had stopped requesting him anymore for doing some work because he didn't want to do any job; though he used to work at a restaurant before getting married to with Simran. Sahil's hobby was to cook different varieties of cuisine.

Simran took out her mobile phone from her purse and called up Sahil while walking on the road. They were walking by one side of the road. It was very difficult to get a taxi from there at that time. They were walking towards the railway station.

"Hey, Naina! Simran, stop," Tina was calling them from far away. Simran was talking over the phone. Naina looked back and saw Tina was running on the road. She told her to slow down as they stopped walking. They waited near the signal for Tina. Tina came near them.

She was breathing very fast and excited to tell her story. "You know, no one knocked on my door. I opened the door for asking beer because no one came after pressing the bell three times. So, I opened the door and found no one in the corridor. There was pin drop silence everywhere.

"I told the customer to run away immediately. He somehow wore his pants and then got down from the window, holding the shirt in his hand. You should have seen his face. My God." She started laughing.

"And you?" Naina asked.

"I followed him. I let him get down first so that I could fall on him and save my leg from breaking." She laughed loud. Everything seemed so funny after managing a safe escape from the police.

"But why did you get down from the window?"

"The front gate was closed by that time. All ran away. The whole building was empty."

"Okay."

"Where you both are going?"

"I am going to Simran's place."

"Okay. I will have to go to the guest house. Let's see who else joins me there."

Simran was standing at a little distance from them and talking over the phone. She finished talking and came near them. Looking at Tina, she said, "Tina, would you like to come with us **at** my home?"

"Hey, that will be great," Tina agreed and said, "I will buy drinks and Naina can buy food."

"I will place the order for food in some restaurant after we reach there," Naina said.

"Tonight, you both are my guests," Simran said, "I already told Sahil to make some special cuisine."

"Okay but we can have that with drinks as starters. I will order for the dinner," Naina said.

"Okay, that's fine," Simran said.

The railway station was not very far from their building. They reached the station. Naina and Tina had to buy tickets. Simran had a first class pass for the train. But they went in the second class ladies compartment together because Naina and Tina had got the tickets for second class. They got down at Andheri station. The station was too crowded. They came out of the station and got into an auto.

Simran told the driver, "Bhaiya, Char bungalow, MHADA."

Tina said, "Bhaiya, please stop at some wine shop on the way."

"Okay, madam," he said and started the auto.

He stopped his auto near a wine shop. Tina got down for getting drinks. She came back with two full bottles of

Blender's Pride. "If we need more, we shall buy one more bottle later at night," she said.

They reached Simran's house. Sahil opened the door for them and entered the kitchen.

"Hi, Sahil! What are you making so special? Nice smell," Naina said.

"I am trying a new recipe, cheese with vegetables and spices," Sahil said, while cooking.

"Simran said that Naina doesn't eat meat. So, I am making vegetarian food today."

"Is it so? I am really afraid! First time you are making it. Hope we will enjoy the taste," Naina mocked.

"I am really honoured. You have so much faith in my cooking." He giggled.

Naina and Tina sat on a cane sofa that was kept in the common space between room, kitchen and dining. Simran said she was going to take a shower so they could start drinking. But Naina told her that they would wait because they too needed to be fresh and later together they would drink. Then she asked Sahil to place the order for the food.

After the order was placed, Sahil told that the kids would be writing exams next day so better not to play music. Guddu and Tinni were studying in the other room. He then got cold drinks and water. After getting fresh, Naina and Tina were sitting on the sofa and talking. Sahil got some cheese and vegetables garnished with lettuce and lemon for them on a few plates.

Naina tasted some vegetables. Taste was awesome. "Yummy! It's just too good."

"Thanks, Naina. Actually, today is Thursday so I had to cook vegetarian only. We eat vegetarian food on Thursday and Saturday."

"But why do you eat vegetarian food on Thursday and Saturday only?" Naina enquired.

"We pay homage to Laxmi Devi and Saturn on these days. Thursday is the day of Jupiter, the planet which represents Guru. Some people don't eat meat on Tuesday, the day of Bajrang Bali," Sahil said.

"You know Sahil, if you stop eating meat, you should stop it totally."

"We cannot stop eating meat totally. It is so difficult to quit non-vegetarian food," Simran said. "Nothing will change by stopping eating animals on Thursday or Saturday or Tuesday. In the form of meat, you are consuming the energy of anxieties, pain, fear, violence which makes you fearful, painful, violent and negative because you get your energy from the food you eat.

You won't have peace of mind consuming the energy of pain and violence. Your energy level will be at your lower chakras of the body. You will remain concerned only about eating, sleeping, mating and fighting for small reasons.

"You are eating the dead body of an animal. A dead body is being served on your plate to be eaten. You mix all kinds of spices to suppress the smell of their blood and flesh to make it eatable. When someone dies within the family or friends, you go to the crematorium for burning the dead body of the person and after coming back from there, you make yourselves clean and then you enter your house.

"But your house itself is like a crematorium where the dead bodies of animals are getting burnt and cooked. You think animals are small, so no problem to cook and eat their dead bodies. But you don't think about the soul present in them is the same what we have within us. The same soul may take birth in a human body in its next birth.

"You may stop it on Thursday or Saturday but the truth will not change. Will God be happy if you eat pain, fear, anxieties, helplessness and sufferings on Sunday or Monday? Or the animals will feel less pain if they are killed on other week days? Think about it logically. All you need to do is to cut your greed, envy, false ego, anger, deep attachment and be a devotee of the God."

"Saturn punishes us."

"We suffer our own karma; we must rectify ourselves internally. Saturn delays things."

"Do you have knowledge about planets? I mean astrology?" Sahil asked.

"Astrology helps you in understanding the journey of your soul. We are under planetary guidance all the time because we are also the same cosmic energy. It's about the reflection of our action what we do, that we get. We and our actions are just a part of the cosmic energy and law, happening since infinity,"

Naina said.

"But small tiny gemstones on our fingers can change the huge planet's position, movements and action and our destiny too," Tina said in a flat tone.

"Gemstones cannot change destiny because only our present actions make our destiny for our next lives. Whether you wear a gemstone or not, things will happen irrespective of that. It doesn't mean things will happen on its own, you only will have to work to make things happen physically. But you will work in that direction which is there in your destiny," Naina said.

"But you just said, all our actions are influenced by the planets and our actions are predestined. SoSo, we are not independent to perform action on our own," Simran said.

"Yes, everything is happening in perfect mathematical order. According to our character, we perform actions and face situations how we are destined to face. We have illusion of free will but we are not free to act in the universe. You have to use your hands for cooking, for writing. You have to use your legs for running; you have to use your mouth for talking or eating.

"You even extend your hand to take the glass of water and use your mouth to sip the drink, right? So, the movements of our body parts that we make to do things, those movements are our actions in the materialistic level of Maya by gross body. You have to think and make plans using your brain.

"Our thoughts are the action of the subtle body. We are performing actions using our body and mind being influenced and regulated by the planets. Lord Krishna after removing Arjuna's illusion, told him to take actionact according to his own wish, he only explained him the truth. He did not force Arjuna to do anything.

"But he also mentioned that ultimately Arjuna would fight because of his Kshatriya nature. His Kshatriya nature would make him fight the battle to restore Dharma. We all do all the work as per our nature. We are already programmed to do what we are doing.

"So, we will be influenced most by the planets but ultimately, it is our subtle and gross body movement which is called action. When we evolve ourselves, change internally as human beings and imbibe the good qualities of planets, then we receive the blessings of the Demigods of the ruling planet," Naina said.

Tina asked, "If we are predestined to do everything then why are you telling us to change internally? The change is not in our hands, we are being controlled like puppets as it happens in a video game! How will we change ourselves?"

"There are three ways to understand it. One, read Gita to understand the way of living, to understand how to function in physical world by correcting your actions using your free will at the mundane level of Maya.

"Two, read Gita to elevate your spiritual consciousness to realise God and live like a yogi. You will get all your answers in it.

Three, if you want to understand in more detail, then, study astrology. You will realise, everything happens in divine order which is called destiny."

"But why do you think that gemstones do not work?" Simran asked.

"To get good result of planets, we need to raise our vibrations by increasing Satvik qualities within us. These gemstones are dead matters. Stones do not have their own live Satvik, Rajasik or Tamasik qualities to influence nature. You can raise your vibration and be connected with the higher realm by your own good qualities and karma.

"So many people are cutting and polishing gemstones every day, their lives remain the same. People enter into the deep mines to excavate, look at their lives, how helpless they are. The gemstones look so beautiful but who makes them valuable and beautiful? Are their lives beautiful and valuable too?

"We should take planets as our mirror, the action we have performed, those reactions are reflected. So, we can't expect to get good result at the cost of innocent people's blood and sweat. Mostly negative energies like greed, envy, sufferingssufferings, and pain are associated with lucrative gemstones.

"But I don't mean to say, these energies are the energy of gemstones. Stones are actually neutral and don't affect planetary actions in any way. Planet acts according to their transits and movements in the sky. And we get result of that and we act according to the periods of planet that we go through.

"Even if you talk about superficial remedies, those are of little help too. Remedies give a positive faith that by doing this or by doing that, problem will be over. Until and unless we change from within as human beings, until we change our karma and thoughts, nothing will change.

"The more we indulge in remedies or gemstones, we ignore karma, the more we indulge in gemstones and remedies, we become narrow minded. We find shortcut to pay back karma. It doesn't happen. We have to understand the planets and their roles in our lives. Rather than trying for gemstones or remedies, we must study about the planets, houses, signs and nakshatras.

"I can give you one example from our basic Kalpurusha chart, the ascendant of the first house is Aris, ascendant ruler is Mars. Ascendant is our intelligence and as well as our physical body. Mars is the planet of action and fiery energy within us. The ascendant ruler of our basic chart Mars gets exalted in the tenth house.

"Exalted means the planet is happiest when he is positioned there. It does not mean we will get our desired result. We will get the result, bad or good depending upon our own past life karma. We can be happy and listen to sad songs, right? We can be happy and we can go for trekking in the mountain and tolerate obstacles and pain.

"We can be happy and eat sugar free, boiled vegetables and do fasting to maintain our body. We can be happy and go to the gym to exercise and tolerate body pain. So not necessarily an exalted planet will give us good result all the time according to our desire which we think is good.

"Exalted planets may make us work harder to reach our goal. Exalted planets make us aware and positive. Satvik qualities are more within us when we have exalted planets. Result of exalted planet depends upon so many things like the house placement based on your ascendant, lordship, conjunction with other planets, aspect, the position of the planet in other divisional chart, etc.

"The ascendant ruler Mars gets exalted in the tenth house, the house of action, status, name, fame, etc. Mars gets its directional strength in tenth house. The sign in the tenth house according to the basic chart is

Capricorn. This sign is ruled by Saturn, the planet of action.

Planet of action is getting exalted in the sign of another action ruling planet. Now you see how our intelligence and body is related with action," Naina stopped as the doorbell rang.

"Maybe the food has come," Simran said.

"Wait, I will see," Sahil said and went to open the door. He came back with parcels and the bill. Naina looked at the bill and paid the amount.

"Huh, lots of food Naina, you have ordered," Sahil said and kept the parcels on the table.

"We can have some now, hot and fresh," she said.

Chapter 12

Tina's phone was ringing. Looking at the screen, she said, "It's Maahi." She picked up her call. They heard just Tina's side.

"Hello!"

-

"Oh, when?"

-

"We are at Simran's house at Andheri now. We had to run away."

-

"Are you safe?"

-

"Okay, you reach home, will talk later." Tina cut the call.

She kept her phone on the centre table. There were crispy baby corn and Gobi Manchurian balls on the plates. They were chewing snacks and sipping at their drinks while talking. Tina's phone call created perturbation in the room.

"What happened?" Simran asked, "Did something happen at Maahi's workplace?"

"There was a police raid, ten females and two service boys were arrested," Tina announced dramatically.

They were shocked by the news and murmured among themselves.

"Now, their building will remain closed for a few months," Naina said.

"Even our building was closed for almost three months last year," Tina said.

"Pratiksha, Sonali and I were arrested," Naina said.

"Hey! Had you even been in jail?" Sahil asked.

"They call it correction home, not jail," Naina said.

"How many days you stayed there?" Sahil asked.

"Twenty-one days," Naina said.

"Oh really! But what happened exactly? How did you get caught?" Sahil asked as he sipped at his whiskey.

"Couldn't you just run faster?" Simran said.

"I didn't get any chance to run away. Pratiksha, Sonali, and I were actually handed to the police so that the rest of the people could be saved from getting arrested," Naina said.

"What? But why you three?" Sahil asked.

"That I realised later," Naina said.

"What happened exactly? Tell us the story,"

"Well, let me go back to that evening," Naina said as she took a large sip of her drink.

"That evening was normal like other days. The front gate was open and boys were moving around with room services or drinks for the females or the guests. In the mean time, three people, one was a lady among them, came upstairs in the hall directly and stood straight, eyes moving and rolling on everything and on every corner of the room. A gush of chilling current passed through my spine……."

"Oh, so no one was being informed about them?" Simran asked, interrupting Naina.

"It seemed so," Naina said.

"Then what happened?" Simran asked.

"Okay, let me tell you in detail." Naina went back to that evening of last year and told them

the story. They listened in silence.

***

Veena was taken aback by their sudden presence in civil dress. Females got frozen with fear while sitting on the benches. They looked down, folding their hands, placing them between their knees. Anika, Nisha, Pinky, Sweety and Aarti began to cry.

Sunil came and stood in front of them like an obedient student standing in front of the principal. Looking at them, he mumbled, "Sir, madam, you all, how come suddenly?" Sunil had no more words. He lowered his head.

"Tell all your staff to keep quiet. Go and sit in the police van below," One of them said.

Sanjay came upstairs. Taking them in a corner, he spoke with them. After some time, the cops agreed to take only three females with them. But there was a catch. They wanted to arrest Veena along with three females. If Veena had to surrender, she would go to jail with the charges of running the prostitution racket. Sanjay had no other option but to agree. Naina, Pratiksha, Sonali, and Veena were taken to the local police station straightaway. They spent the night in the lock up. One of the managers from the adjacent building, named Sailesh, came to meet them. He got sweet lime juice for all. After the statement had been given, Sailesh talked with them for some time.

"How was the juice?" Sailesh asked.

"It was sweet." Naina smiled, "Thank you."

Pratiksha and Sonali were angry and annoyed on Sanjay because he was the one to select and hand them to the police. Why didn't he send somebody else? Why they? They had served in that building since so many years and that was what they got in return. They were cursing the managers and everyone whoever came within their radar.

"We are here in the lock up and you are asking, how was the juice? When will you take us out from here?" Pratiksha asked furiously.

"Don't worry. Keep cool, okay," Sailesh said.

"How many days we have to be here?" Sonali asked.

"Minimum twenty-one days. But if you get punishment, then one year."

"Sailesh ji, will you let us be inside for one year?" Sonali had her tears ready to roll down her cheeks.

"Come on girls, how can you think that we will let you be inside for one year? We will then apply in the high court if you are not released within twenty-one days," Sailesh said.

Sonali's tears fell on the floor.

"Don't worry. Our owner will do all the expenses and we will try our best to take you all out within twenty-one days," Sailesh assured.

Now it was Pratiksha's turn. She too brought enough tears in her eyes to wet the floor.

After all this was over, Sailesh asked, "I will have to call up your home. Do you all have your identity cards here?"

"Yes," they said in unison.

"I will have to call your parents or husbands. Tell me whom should I call up? Give me their numbers. Either parents or husband anyone. They will have to come here to meet the magistrate in the court. By tomorrow, they will have to be here," Sailesh said.

"Sailesh ji, I can't give my parents' number," Sonali said, "They don't know that I am working as a prostitute here. My father is paralysed, totally bed ridden. My mother looks after him. She will not be able to come. They stay in a remote village. They don't have any idea about all this. They are very simple people,"

Sonali said as she again accumulated a good amount of tears in her eyes.

"Then give me your husband's number. Otherwise, it is not possible for me to proceed in your case," Sailesh said impatiently.

"I don't have a husband. I just have a boyfriend," Sonali said, while wiping her tears.

"As usual, you keep boyfriends to spend your money on them. What is the use of keeping such boyfriends? If you would have married him, now he would have been of some use. Who will prove your identity now? Your mother has to come, it is a must. You can tell your sister to look after your father," Sailesh said, a bit excited and annoyed at the same time by Sonali's innocence.

"But they will die if they come to know that I am into prostitution," Sonali said.

"Your parents will come to know; I can't help it. Give me the phone number," Sailesh said.

Then he looked at Naina and Pratiksha, "Whose numbers will you give? They will have to come here and stay."

"Where will they stay? Who will bear their expenses?" Pratiksha said.

"Our owner will provide them with a guest house and two times food."

"How many days would they need to stay here?" Pratiksha asked.

"How can I say that now? It may take twenty-one days to four months or more."

Naina gave her husband's number. Pratiksha gave her mother's number. Sailesh had got

towel, tooth brush, night dress, soap, toothpaste, etc. with him in three bags. They would need them in the correction home.

Next day, they were taken for medical check-up in hospital. It was a mandatory process to check if someone was below eighteen years. Then they were taken to the court. In the court, it really took a long time. Sanjay already called up their homes. They were supposed to be in the court that day.

Naina had a habit of smoking cigarettes. She was becoming irritated without smoking. The only thing in her mind was to get some tobacco. She asked Sanjay, "When my husband will come? How long will we have to wait?"

"Why? You need your cigarettes?" Sanjay said.

"Sanjay ji, since yesterday I didn't smoke a single cigarette, you know how tough it is for me; my brain shall collapse now," Naina said.

"You people will not change, huh! Just earn and then spend the money on smoking and drinking. I keep telling you to save money. These are your hard-earned money but you never listen. You spend money on addiction or on boyfriend," Sanjay said.

"Days are dull without cigarettes Sanjay ji; you will not understand."

Sanjay didn't realise her deep remorse. He was not impacted at all.

"Don't give me excuses. Now, what will you do inside? There you will not get anything," Sanjay said in a flat tone.

Naina was tension free. "Cool Sanjay ji, I will get tobacco there," she replied.

Sanjay burst out into laughter. "You will never change, Naina."

Sonali said, "Hey Naina, you see your husband is there standing at the gate. Pratiksha's mother is also there. Let us go there." Then she looked at Sanjay and said, "Sanjay ji, call my mother once more."

"I already spoke to her; she is on her way," Sanjay said.

"Okay, thanks," Sonali said.

"You know how much tension I have to go through when you people are caught," Sanjay said, "From arranging money to talking with police, courtcourt, and your guardians, I handle everything. You will just be inside but I will keep running outside. Moreover, the building will remain closed now for many days."

Sonali and Pratiksha's anger and frustration towards Sanjay became little less after they heard the other part of the story. They realised, it was painful for them and for others too, it was not sweet. It was a hard time for everybody working there. They reached near the gate of the court.

Sanjay said, "Girls, listen carefully. You and your guardian both need to say the same thing in the court. So, talk and discuss well what you are going to say to the magistrate. Have a proper rehearsal, okay?"

"Okay," they said in unison.

Within a few minutes, they got busy in their discussion. After the court's procedures got over, Veena had to go back in the lock up under the police remand.

Sonali, Pratiksha, and Naina got into the police van, which would take them to the correction home. They had to bid their family good bye.

Sonali, after meeting her mother at the court, was feeling depressed. She told them earlier that she worked at a garment shop and then meeting her mother at the court with the charges of prostitution, shook her mother from inside. The lady police patted Sonali's back and said,

"Don't worry Sonali, stay there for few weeks, your managers will try their best to take you from there as soon as possible."

Sonali said, "Madam, you know that within a span of three months to one year, we will get out from the correction home and will get back to the profession again. Then why do you arrest us?"

"This is my duty, my dear. I am just doing my job."

"But why do you arrest us? Have we committed any crime?"

"Your profession is against the social norms."

"Madam, then why don't you do something about the cause of the prostitution? Why there Is so much of illiteracy and unemployment? What will we eat? What will we wear? Where will we stay? Why there is so much of sexuality in men that they can't control and may rape someone! But instead, they come to us to touch our body and fulfil their desire.

"If we don't exist in the society then where those people, who touch women's back or breasts in the public bus, will go? Where that man will go who has a lusty eye on his sister-in-law or on the maidservant or on the neighbour's wife? Where that person will go who is frustrated to have sex?

"Madam, have you ever thought how the sex workers are tolerating so much? So many drunk and difficult customers come. We only know how we handle them. I am not telling that I came to serve the people for helping society, no; I came in prostitution for my own personal reasons. I am not justifying my job. I am just telling you the facts. We give most importance to relations, to family, to love. For them, we sacrifice everything."

The lady police said, "We have problems and limitations in our society. Still, it is not the right thing to do."

"What is the right thing to do, madam? Is it right to commit suicide without food , money and shelter?" Sonali said.

The other two cops were silent. They didn't take part in the conversation.

"Madam, customer's family don't come to know about them after the raid," Sonali said.

"Customers have name, fame, and respect in the society. They will lose their respect if their family come to know about them," the lady police said.

"Oh okay, they have respect, if we wouldn't have been there to fulfil their sexual urge, then soon they would have lost their respect by committing some immoral activities within the society. In spite of having a wife at home, they meet us for fulfilling their sexual desires, that time they don't lose respect. They lose respect when people come to know about their truth. Then what is the definition of respect? Is it all about covering the truth with lies?"

"People, mostly are hypocrites, at least I have met them, to be precise," Pratiksha said.

No one commented. Naina looked outside and kept looking at the roads and traffic of Mumbai.

Chapter 13

The car reached the correction home. The compound was huge. They got down from the car. The lady police asked, "Have you taken all your things?"

"Yes, madam," they said in unison.

"Good, take care and be in discipline."

Naina, Pratiksha, and Sonali got down from the car. Main gate was locked. Few lady home guards were there at the gate. One of them got the keys and opened the gate. They walked inside slowly. The lady constable went inside the office to complete some official formalities. Naina, Pratiksha, and Sonali entered the correction home after being checked by a lady home guard. There was a big hall room. Within moments, they were mobbed by the women who were inside the home. Few children were also there. Their clothes, floor, the dirty blankets and torn mattresses were so gloomy.

Sonali's eyes filled with tears to see such an environment. "What a horrible place! What correction are they doing in this place? Will this correction home correct customer's mind? Or will it correct the financial problems of my life?"

"It will correct your nature and guide your mind so that you perform better actions," Naina said.

"And where those actions will take place? Are you going to open some new office and provide me with a job there after your vibrations are raised here?"

Naina didn't say anything in reply. She requested one of the women there to show her where the bathroom was. One of them went with her. After coming from the bathroom, she saw, Sonali and Pratiksha were sitting in a corner along with three other women. Mattresses were scattered here and there. Tube lights were on but the gloomy light couldn't remove the inside darkness of the room.

Women were divided into small groups. Few were playing some board games. Few people were playing cards, one of them was making tobacco, hiding under her clothes. Children were running around and playing. She counted the children; they were total five.

She went and sat beside her friends.

"Hi, I am Naina." She introduced herself with the other three women sitting there.

The eldest of them introduced herself as Nazia. "She is Selima and she is Shabana," Nazia said.

She smiled at them.

"Naina, do you have tobacco in your mouth?" Pratiksha asked.

"Yes. That was the reason I wanted to go to the bathroom." Naina smiled, "But you know it is not smooth like smoking cigarettes. It is burning within my mouth."

"But how did you get it here?" Pratiksha was taken aback.

Naina blinked her eyes. "I bought it when my husband came to meet me and we all went to have lunch in the restaurant. There I went in the bathroom and placed it inside my dress."

Pratiksha exhaled a deep breath of relief through her mouth. "Good that she didn't check properly," she said, "Next time when you make tobacco for yourself, give me also some. That is needed in such a clumsy environment. I will soon go mad, I think."

"Where are you from?" Naina asked Nazia.

"We three are from Bangladesh," Nazia said.

"Okay, when did you come here?" She asked casually.

Nazia said, "I came here six years back, Selima came seven years back. Shabana is also here from last six years."

Now that was a shock. Sonali almost screamed, "What! This is unbelievable. Girls are released within a few months, maximum one year that also if she has been given punishment."

Naina and Pratiksha couldn't talk for some time. Then Naina spoke, her voice was low, she said, "Few girls were arrested from our building, they were released soon."

"Was anyone of them from Bangladesh?" Selima asked.

"Many of them were from Bangladesh. They might have made their Indian identity card. I am not sure but whenever there used to be some police problem, our managers used to shift them in the guest house so that the police cannot reach them," Pratiksha said.

"We didn't have any identity card when we were arrested. So, we are inside this home from so many years," Nazia said.

"But where are your family, aren't they trying to take you out from here? They should come here with all your documents and produce them in the court," Naina said.

Selima said, "They are trying but it seems to be difficult. My husband was working as a farmer. He used to work on other people's land. Sometimes he had work, sometimes he did not have. Seeing my family starving, I trusted a broker who told me that I can earn good money and save my family from starving.

"He would take care of rest everything. Within fifteen days of coming to India, I got arrested. I didn't have any money then. The broker said he would take the first month's salary and then from the next month, I would get money. But before that, I reached here."

Sonali asked, "Who all are there in your family? Do you have children?"

"I have two sons. I haven't seen them from the last seven years. When I came here, my elder son was four years old, younger one was two years old," Selima said.

"They must be missing their mother so much," Naina said.

"Nazia also has one daughter in her village, she saw her six years back and her daughter was only five years old then," Shabana said.

Everybody fell silent. After a few minutes of silence, Prateeksha asked, "Selima, don't your family members try to take you out?"

"They try but we have entered this country without any identity proof, passportpassport, and visa. We got arrested while doing illegal activities, so it is very difficult for us to be released from here. The man, Khaled who brought me in Mumbai, didn't tell me anything. He told me about prostitution but not about any documents. Just think what kind of a person is he! He knew that I was arrested and will not be released from the jail; stillstill, he continues to do the same thing."

Nazia said, "It is very easy to arrest women because police know where to find them to dump within correction home. But they don't know where will they go and get those brokers who take advantage of our hunger and illiteracy."

"But why did you come without passport and visa?" Sonali asked.

"We didn't have much idea about visa and passport then. We were helpless that time and wanted to earn money somehow. You all will be released soon. God knows what will happen to us," Shabana said.

"Shabana, are you all coming for the prayer?" A thin, tall girl was calling them. She looked at Naina and told, "You all can come and join our prayer in the next room." She didn't wait for their reply, she went back.

"What's her name?" Sonali asked.

"She is Mallika. She is here from last two years now," Shabana said.

"Is she also from Bangladesh?"

"No, she is from India but I don't know why is she still inside."

"Doesn't she have her family?"

"No, she says there is no one in her family."

"Oh."

"Do you all want to come for the prayer?"

"What prayer is this?"

"I don't understand the language, there is one lady named Misha, she is from Ukraine, she is here inside from last one year. She taught us this prayer. We all sing together and pray for our family. We pray so that we can be released soon from here." In the next room, fifty or more women were sitting in a circle for prayer. Sonali, Pratiksha and Naina also joined them. Some of them were crying while praying. They were inside this home from so many months or years without their children and family. There was pain and sorrow in the air.

They came out of the hall room slowly and sat outside in the corridor. They could see the kitchen from there. Pale yellow light was coming from the kitchen window and was falling on the ground. Few ladies were preparing dinner.

After few minutes of silence, Sonali said, "I was crying so much. After seeing them, I forgot to cry. We will be out from here within one year. But look at them, they are here from years, no one is there to support them or to take them out. They are also mothers, wives and above all, they are human beings."

Few other women came outside in the corridor and joined them. After some time, Nazia Came to call them for dinner.

"What is the time now, Nazia?" Naina asked.

"It is nine pm now. Let us go and stand in the queue for dinner."

"Okay."

They entered the kitchen. The kitchen was noisy. They took little food and came outside and sat in the corridor. They were not feeling like eating anything. Shabana and Selima were with them. Shabana took some food and went in the room and came back with an empty plate.

Sonali asked, "What did you do with the food?"

"I saved my food, now I will get one more plate of food. Later, we will eat in the night. Sometimes in the night, we can't sleep and then we feel hungry. AlsoAlso, the children ask for more food sometimes."

"This is very pathetic Shabana, how you all are living your life here?" Naina said. Her eyes were moist.

***

The atmosphere of the correction home was depressing. Every passing moment was suffocating, though playing Ludo and chewing tobacco supplied some breathing air. The place was like some stable where human beings lived from months and years without knowing the reason for living. Many women who were there from a long time were making various plans for breaking out from the home, though nothing of that sort happened till they were there.

***

One afternoon, Nazia got a handful of rice grain from the kitchen.

Naina asked, "What is this for?"

"Come and sit here. I will show you," she said and called Sonali, Pratiksha, Selima and others.

They all sat in a circle. Nazia heaped the rice grains and told everyone to take little from that heap and then count the grains. Thus, they will come to know how soon they were going to be released. This game gave them some hope of freedom.

***

"I saw total five kids. Whose kidskids, are they?" Pratiksha asked.

"Three of them were born here. Their mothers were caught pregnant. And the other two have come with their mother because no one was there to look after them."

Pratiksha asked, "Where are their fathers?"

Naina said, "Nobody knows where they are. In the area where sex workers work for low budget, customers don't want to use condoms. So, there is high chance that women become HIV positive or they become pregnant. In those low budget areas, there is no cleanliness.. In the same room, people eat, urinate, take bath, and have sex. The bed sheets and pillow covers are not changed for months. They use stored water, which is a birthplace of mosquitoes."

Pratiksha said, "These kids within the correction home are not getting proper nutrition, not even any education."

After some time, a home guard told them, "All go inside and sleep. Whoever wants to use bathroom may go. After this, no one will be allowed to go to the bathroom till six o'clock in the morning."

Next morning, they got up hearing the home guard's voice. Naina opened her eyes, looking at the big clock, time was six am. She went in the bathroom. Water was running very slow. She went to the kitchen. Tea and breakfast were being served. There was a television in the kitchen.

Some of the women were watching a movie on the television. She took some tea and bread and sat on one of the benches that were kept outside the kitchen. Pratiksha and Sonali came after some time and joined her for the breakfast.

***

In the afternoon, they were playing Ludo. Mallika came to call everyone. She said to go near the office room for some people were distributing oranges and biscuits. They went and stood in the queue; till their turn came, the biscuits got over.

Nazia said, "The office people keep first for them, then the rest are served to us. That is why these things get over."

"So many people in the country are corrupted from head to toe yet living lavish life. Then why only helpless, illiterate, and hungry people are to suffer?" Sonali commented.

No one replied.

Finally, the day came when Naina got released after twenty-one days. Sonali and Pratiksha cried their heart out when she was released early. Few of the women gave their phone numbers to call up at their homes.

Sonali and Pratiksha were released after four months but they had to spend another two months in some other correction home of West Bengal before they were finally released.

Chapter 14

Naina and Zarina came to meet Sheena who had a train in the evening that would take her to her hometown. Sheena was only sixteen years old when she got married. Her husband left and went somewhere after a son was born to her. Sheena became like a burden at her parent's house.

Her aunty, who was working at a brothel in Mumbai, brought Sheena to the same place where she was working. Sheena had no other option other than working as a prostitute. She requested her brothers just to keep her son with them; she would send money every month for looking after her child. Her brothers happily agreed. Since then, Sheena was working in the brothels of Mumbai.

Entering her room, they found she was still busy with her last last-minute packing her bags and luggage were scattered all around the room. Clothes and gift items were dumped on the bed. She was dumping too many clothes in a bag and struggling to pull the zipper.

"My God, Sheena, how long will you take to finish your packing?" Naina said.

"Almost done, little is left. Come, sit," Sheena said, tapping on the bed. Then she took out some clothes from her cupboard and kept those in another bag.

"Zarina, help me please in packing the bags," Sheena said.

Zarina smiled. "Why didn't you call me before? All your packing would have been finished by now."

"But why are you taking so many bags?" Naina said.

Sheena looked delighted. She said, "I go home once in six months. I take gifts for everyone In my family."

"Great!" Naina said, "But how will you go alone with so many bags? Should I come with you to the station?"

"Thanks, Naina," she said, "You don't worry, Darshan is coming. He will drop me at the station."

"Okay, that's good," Naina said, "How many days will you be staying at home?"

"Just two months."

"Your son must be very happy now," Zarina said, while struggling to pack the bags perfectly.

"Yes, he is very happy. He is counting days."

"Why don't you get your son here for some days? You can arrange his staying at Meghna's place," she suggested.

"Next year, I will get my son here. We will be staying together with Darshan," Sheena said, a smile on her face.

"Is this the reason you gave money to Darshan from your savings?" Zarina asked.

"I helped him with money because ultimately, we will be staying together."

"When Darshan comes to meet you here; you only pay the money to the manager. He doesn't pay for anything," Zarina said.

"He is saving money for buying an apartment. After that we will stay together," Sheena said. She was beaming.

"Congratulations Sheena, we wish soon you go out from this place and live your dreams,"

both said and hugged her.

Zarina and Naina arranged the things properly and packed her bag nicely. Sheena's phone rang. Looking at her phone, she said, "Darshan is calling up and he is down there. I have to go now." She pressed the bell switch near the bed.

Arun came in the room within minutes. "Did you call, madam?" He asked.

"Yes Arun, please help me carrying my luggage below. Darshan is standing there."

"Okay, madam." Then he looked at Naina and said, "Madam, you have customer in room number five. Sunil ji's customer."

"Have you given the room service and drinks?" She enquired.

"Yes, all is done. I was looking for you in the other rooms. You can go and lock the door,"

Arun said as he picked up Sheena's luggage.

***

Room number five was one of the best rooms there, decorated with colourful lights and wall size mirrors. Lalit was looking at his mobile phone. Seeing Naina, he smiled. "Hey Naina, a warm welcome to you, how are you doing?" He greeted.

"I am fine, what about you?" Naina said, sitting on the bed.

"I am doing okay," he said as he ran his fingers through his hair. He paused a little and said,

"With age, so many things change you know; just feeling little tired mentally and physically."

"How old are you?" Naina said, "Let me guess umm, around fifty maybe?" Though she had sixty-five in mind but she just wanted to make him feel good.

He laughed loud. "Do I really look like fifty? I mean, I take it as a complement and thank you for that,"

Naina smiled nicely. "You do look like fifty."

"I am sixty-three years old now."

"You are young at heart," she said. She was just trying to make his mood light. Lalit was a well-behaved person. She had been with him two times before. His fantasy was to see women acting in the role of different professionals who would make love to him. Sometimes, he would say to act as secretary of his office. Sometimes, he would say to act as an air hostess, sometimes a model or the girl next door. This was actually tough for Naina because she was a very bad actor and an introvert kind of a person. First time she was so confused what to act as. Then Lalit suggested **her** to change her jeans and wear a sari and act as a next-door wife.

That was the first time she was with Lalit. Second time, she had to act as a fresher who went for a job interview and finally ended up sleeping with the employer. Naina was thinking what he might tell her to be. She finished her first peg and started to have the second one. Lalit was silent unlike how he used to be before.

"What happened to you? Why are you so quiet?" Naina asked.

"Nothing." He gave a faint smile and said, "You tell me what you are going to be for me today. Please tell me freely, don't hesitate, okay?"

"Let me be your friend, only friend and nothing else. We can have talks and discussions on different topics," Naina said.

"Good. Actually, I wanted to talk with someone who would understand."

"You can tell me."

"I didn't go to any brothel from last six months. I and my wife went to our daughter's place a few months back. When I was there, I had a guilty feeling. I was thinking that I have slept with so many women in my whole life and my wife doesn't know anything about it. What if my son-in-law is also doing the same? This thought was not giving me peace.

"How wrong was I to sleep with so many women? Looking at my son-in-law, I developed a complex feeling of guilt. I was in a dilemma for the last three months at home. And then I decided to come here for the last time. This is so wired that I can't share this feeling with anyone else," he said as he let out a deep breath.

"You are feeling insecure about your daughter. But this is totally from your point of view because you slept with females, your son-in-law may not be like you at all. You tell women to act in different roles. One reason may be, you do not want to have sex with a prostitute, so you tell us to be someone else.

"Or the other reason may maybe you want to have sex with different women in the society but you cannot do that. So, you tell us to act in different roles and fulfil your desire. Now you tell me which reason is true for you?"

"The last one and it started with watching pornography. There I saw different techniques of enjoying sex. That is one reason to come here and satisfy my lust. What I watched in the pornography, I tried the same thing here with you all. I liked it too but now I feel guilty for whatever I have done, I have lost my self-respect. This is even an insult of their profession as well as an insult of women," Lalit said.

"Whatever happened in your life, it happened due to lack of love, respect, and compassion. You never tried to live for a higher purpose. You never had any higher queries in life, so you just lived your instinct. Your intelligence drove you in wrong direction. We all go through such situation because of our ignorance and selfish desires.

"There are some customers who while having sex here, imagine us as their friends or someone else. Some people come here when their wives are pregnant. Some customers come due to some fantasy which they can't fulfil at home with their wives. Some people come whose girlfriends don't let them have sex before marriage. Some people come who has no one to have sex." Naina stopped and asked, "You know why people are craving so much for fulfilling lust?"

"Why?" Lalit asked her back.

"Because our thoughts are limited within the sensual bodily pleasures only; we have limited ourselves within our body. So, our mind is confined within sensual bodily thoughts. We establish the idol of God and limit him only within the idol. We don't want to know about yoga, Pranayama, and scriptures.

"Eyes see opposite sex, tongue wants non-vegetarian food; skin wants to touch opposite sex, so, we earn money to achieve all these and fulfil our desires. Later we feel left out, depressed, guilty, lonely, and violent. We are not in peace. Good that you are analysing your actions. You have just started your journey in the path of knowing yourself," Naina said.

"I was thinking of joining some meditation course. You just spoke my mind," Lalit said.

"You should join meditation course; it will reconstruct your thought process towards positivity. You will learn to focus on what is essential in life, **There you will learn Pranayam which will channelise the flow of prana or the life force.**

Lalit nodded his head. Naina thought she should talk some more with him to make him talk more and clear his mind so that he could think positive about life. She asked, "What went wrong between you both that you suddenly became so desperate to enjoy sex outside marriage?"

"Quarrels started between us. We started finding faults in each other. The warmth of our love was totally missing just within few years of our marriage. Slowly, physical attraction was gone but my sexual urges were high. Naturally, I started looking for sexual enjoyment outside. I have enough money to spend too, which is also one big reason to come here and spend," Lalit said.

"This is the basic problem you see; we people use love as a tool to enjoy good sex. So once the sexual attraction is over, love is also gone. Our innermost darkest desires suppress our true feelings of love. Love is unconditional. Love is deeper than that of the ocean, love is vastthan that of the sky, love is that feeling which is like an ever-lightening sparkle that always shines bright in mind.

"We think love is just the attraction which we feel towards the opposite sex. The attraction or infatuation is momentary superficial feelings. Love never fades away. Love awakens our mind. We grow in love and discover the nature of our true self when we both share love, affection and respect for each other. True love brings out the best in each other."

"Why do we lose sexual attraction after few years of marriage? That is the reason we look for enjoyment outside marriage."

"What I have learnt from my experience is, we should be matured enough to understand relations before we get married to someone. We get married with someone who will fulfil our dreams and emptiness and take away our miseries. The other person is also expecting the same from me.

"So, we both are basically empty from within and expecting the other person to fulfil that emotional need. Both are just trying to extract from each other. No one is willing to give, share and sacrifice. Love is about giving but you intended more towards taking, maybe. So you lost your feelings for her.

"When people get married, they give priority to position, money, status in the society, looks, etc. which have nothing to do with love and warmth in the relation. You will naturally lose interest in your partner when the relationship is based on selfish desire. Also, one common reason is we get involved in sexual activities too often with our partner.

"Sexual energy is the most important creative vital force of our body. More we lose this positive energy, the feeling of love goes away, negativity increases. The more we hold this energy within; it will keep us youthful, healthy, energetic, and positive from within. When we know our true self, then we do not look for sexual enjoyment outside marriage."

"What is our true self?"

"Our true self is, we are soul a part of the supreme soul. But our mind is unaware and ignorant about it, so we look for superficial joy outside, we don't know that our soul inside is the eternal consciousness bliss, the source of all knowledge, joyjoy, and happiness. When we understand this, then we don't need to look for momentary superficial pleasure outside.

"In search of superficial joy and happiness, we are entering into more darkness. But to feel this joy within, you need to elevate your consciousness by increasing Satvik qualities in your nature. You have to overcome your negative desires. You should not think negative about your son-in-law.

"Thinking negative thoughts spread more negativity. The more you think negative, the more you will produce negativity in mind. Negativity may start from a small thought but may end up in disaster. Try to appreciate people and find good qualities in them."

"I went on the wrong track." Lalit was looking sad.

Looking at him Naina could feel that he was going through deep regret. She told him, "I am also, in the wrong track of life. Still, I am trying to be a better person every day. Negativity never lets you grow. You said you have enough money to spend, then you should spend your money in doing something constructive for the wellbeing of our society, it will even give you inner fulfilment.

"When you do something good for people or innocent animals, it fills your heart with true feeling of everlasting joy; it gives you a reason to live. It raises your vibrations and consciousness. Think about doing something constructive which will make you feel goodb about yourself again like before.

"Put even much more effort to construct some organisation for the education of helpless and underprivileged children. You will feel youthful when you will be surrounded by young innocent children or anything similar you would like to do for the people or the animals. The joy and happiness on their face will remove all your darkness from your mind.

"You will live your life again with them because it will keep you engaged and involved. It will give you a meaningful life. You have lived a different kind of life, You can also write about your mistakes and regrets and publish a book to create an awareness among the young generations. This will keep you involved in greater purpose."

Lalit's face looked bright. He was smiling, he said, "Good, really a great idea. My daughter and son-in-law are coming home this Diwali and then I will discuss and make some plan with them."

"I am happy for you, Lalit. I wish you all success," Naina said.

"We have been talking for a long time. Let's eat something now. Please call someone and order for some good food."

Naina pressed the bell switch beside the bed.

Chapter 15

"What are your plans for this Diwali? How are you going to celebrate it?" Naina asked, keeping the empty plates aside.

He said, "My grand-daughter had already ordered for lots of fire crackers. Few other relatives will also come. They are excited to burst fire crackers this Diwali."

"But these fire crackers are so bad for the environment," Naina said, "Already our natural environment is so polluted; we again add to it by bursting fire crackers. We think it is only for two days. But the effects and residues of poisonous gases remain in the environment for a long time. Such pollution is extremely bad for our lungs and heart."

"Right but who cares!"

"What environment are we preparing for our next generations to live in? We are polluting air and water. We are using our natural resources excessively, mixing pesticides and worst chemicals in crops and vegetables, cutting trees and forests for making big multi-storied buildings, killing animals, using worst fertilisers in the agricultural land for growing crops. We are just destroying everything."

Taking a pause, Naina said, "Why to talk about air pollution only, the rivers are also getting polluted and stagnant by the chemicals coming out from factories. We, after prayers and rituals, throw the idols of the demigods in lakes and rivers with so much of fun, music and dance. Sometimes I think, is it not an insult of the demigods to throw them in the river?

Have they ever tried throwing demigod's idols or photos at home?" Naina asked his opinion.

Lalit thought for some time and then said, "The joy and fun involved in such idol worship is huge. I am not talking about me now but when I was in my school and college, we had a lot of fun during such celebrations. We used to wait for such programs to get holidays from school. No studies, only fun and enjoyment.

"Buying new clothes, eating outside, drinking alcohol, gossiping with friends, partying in the DJ nights and watching movies; all kinds of fun. Girls used to wear beautiful clothes, their make-up would look so beautiful. It was real fun to watch girls and make friendship with them in those festival days. Total celebration mood. We all become one and united during the celebration times. No rich or no poor."

A faint smile appeared on Naina's face. She said, "When I was in my school days, we friends used to plan for what to wear during the festival days, how to cut hair, which make-up would look the best on us, which gift to buy for friends, which shop to go for buying new clothes, which beauty parlour to go for making us look good; new books would be published, new movie would be released!

"Total festive mood all around in the atmosphere and thus, festival becomes our primary motive. We enjoy the festival. We worship all the demigods for materialistic gains. We discuss among us that Lord Shiva would be happy with little small things and bless us whereas other demigods need much more arrangements and worshipping to be happy and bless us. So, we invest more money and make more superficial arrangements to worship them.

"A person on behalf of us does all the rituals. We then look at the lights or at the decoration of the kiosk. Or we pray for our own material wellbeing. We don't pray to God for other people's happiness. We have no connection or very little inner connection with demigods. We do kiosk hopping, enjoy the gatherings and count how many idols we have visited.

"Enjoying, roaming around, eating outside, and gossiping during such celebrations are the main aim than true devotion for them. You are saying rich and poor become one during such rituals. Then why the poor are on the street and begging food? Why don't they have good clothes or new shoes? Why do we calculate so much while paying bonus to our house or company employees?

"It is like an extra pressure on us to pay bonus to them during such celebrations. We are always trying to extract from others. The simplicity, emotion, love, joy, and devotion that connect us with God, is mostly missing in such artificial and superficial arrangements. These arrangements are not fulfilling us from within with spiritual knowledge. These arrangements have become a total business setup.

"We make our holidays and business plans for those worshipping days. Movies are released during those times to get more business. We go to travel somewhere and use those holidays. Tours and travel business flourish during the festive seasons. Big banners of commercials, and advertisements are displayed everywhere.

"DJ nights, functions and gatherings, competitions are arranged to enjoy and have fun. So, the main purpose of such celebrations is having fun, enjoying holidays and most importantly making business. We go to Kumbh Mela for washing off our sins. By polluting river with our own sin, we cannot get rid of sin.

"We go there to earn merit and virtue. Why don't we correct our own actions instead? We quarrel for small things with our neighbours; we shout on our housemaid for taking extra leave or for asking for extra money, yet we demand unwavering commitment from them. We bargain with a vegetable vendor for even two rupees in the market.

"We fight with each other for the smallest things on the earth like few square feet of land, few rupees or for something which keeps us attached with the karma and never let the soul be free from the birth and death cycle. And then we go and take a bath in Ganga in Kumbh

Mela and make the holy place dirty with all kinds of garbage.

"Instead of washing our sin in Ganga, we should try to keep Ganga as clean as possible. River Ganga has become stagnant and polluted because of us. Keeping Ganga clean will be the real worshipping and paying obeisance to God. We cannot be free from our sins by taking bath in Ganga.

"In Varanasi, people burn the physical body besides river Ganga thinking by burning the physical body, the soul will attain Moksha. We cannot attain Moksha by burning the physical body. Body is physical and perishable so we burn body after death but we forget that soul is carrying karma with it from millions of years.

"Karma goes with the soul in its next birth. Ultimately, our karma will make us free or keep us bound. We pray for our soul's peace and freedom but soul is the everlasting, unchanging eternal consciousness bliss and the part of the supreme almighty God, so always in peace. It is our karma which keeps the soul attached in Maya and away from Moksha."

"What is Moksha"?

"Moksha or liberation means removing ignorance and be free from the miseries and sorrows of mundane materialistic desires. **Moksha is Self- realisation**

"Moksha also means end of delusion, meaning we are not emotionally attached with the material world but doing work as our duty. It happens when we realise the truth within, through self-enquiry and of course, by God's grace."

"Is it possible to proceed towards Moksha in our day to day-to-day life?" Lalit was thoughtful.

"It is possible when we control our senses sincerely trying to keep our mind free from lust, jealousy, greed, anger, etc. When we help each other in the family and at the work place, When we take responsibility and treat people with love and respect, then we follow the moral and ethics taught in our scriptures ages back."

Lalit said, "In present days, there is lack of humanity. So many casts, so many religions, difference between skin colours actually dividing our society. This division within people is not making us united. We hate people easily, love less because of division. We don't respect people for what they are instead we want to prove us better than the other division. False ego and anger are produced within us."

"This happens due to ignorance. There are different kinds of people and they may belong to different race, cast and religion because we all are born to pay certain karma related to that race, cast or religion. We should understand, ultimately, we all are on the same boat, paying back our own respective karma the way it is destined for us. So, there is no point to hate or disrespect anyone for anything."

"If everything is predestined, then what is our own karma? We do something bad because it was there in my karma that I will be bad? Then it's not my fault." Lalit was surprised.

"True, you are performing action according to your nature. You are doing something bad to someone because that person had to receive his part of karma from you in that way. We all are interconnected in such a manner that things are happening in divine order.

"But now, the time has come for you to change your thoughts and focus in life and correct your actions in the mundane level so you are discussing such a topic with me. You know, all these are like part of the game. We all are like actors on the stage of a theatre.

"Destiny and free will are like the two sides of the same coin. Destiny is the ultimate truth and free will is an illusionary truth at the mundane level of Maya. You can understand and realise things as per your own perception. I have tried to explain both the sides."

Naina had to stop, hearing a soft knock on the door.

"Madam, time is up," Suresh called from outside.

Chapter 16

After lunch Ishika, Saloni, Nikita, and Naina were lying on bed in Saloni's room. Saloni was talking with her sister Sazia over the phone.

"Sazia got a new job at an NGO," Saloni said after she finished talking with her.

"Does she like her job?" Nikita asked.

"She likes her job very much," Saloni said.

"That's really nice," Nikita said.

"Hmm, she always wanted to work at some NGO. After studying computers, she is teaching children there," Saloni said. She seemed to feel proud of her sister's achievement.

"This is fantastic. The money you spent for their education is fructifying in a positive way," Nikita said.

"What is your younger brother doing now?" Ishika wanted to know.

"He is supplying surgical instruments into hospitals."

"Okay, when will he marry?"

"He is telling me to settle first and then he will marry. I have told them not to wait for me to get married because I already spent most of my money for raising them. I helped my boyfriend in paying his credit card loans. I have little savings now. I will have to save some

money for my future," Saloni said.

Saloni was the eldest of five brothers and sisters in their family. She was into prostitution from last ten years. Two years ago, she helped her boyfriend to pay all his credit card loans. Just after the loan was paid, her boyfriend changed his mobile number and never showed up. She went into trauma. She stopped taking food, even stopped talking with all of them. Initially, they thought she would be alright within few days. Madam was consoling her like amother. But she was not responding. Whole day and night, she used to remain quiet.

Seeing her condition, madam called up Saloni's mother. Sazia came to Mumbai and took her back to Hyderabad, her home town. Few months later, she got well by psychiatric treatment.

Then she started working again.

Ishika said, "Similar thing happened in my life too." Then she looked at Saloni and said,

"You know everything, I told you."

"I heard from Saloni that you had a very problematic life at your parents' house. Then you loved someone and left your house," Nikita said.

"And he dumped me in a brothel." **Said Ishika.**

Saloni said, "Remember Ishika, he used to come here to take money from you."

"He took almost all my money. Now I am in such a condition that I don't have any place to go. At least in this place, I am safe and getting shelter, that also till I am working here. I don't know where to go after a few years." Ishika was depressed.

Nikita tried to console her. She said, "Our owner will keep you as our madam, you see."

Ishika gave a faint smile. "You know Nikita, working as a madam is not easy. A madam is kept in such brothels for some reason. During the time of police raids, everybody including managers and boys run away. The owner is always behind the screen. The only person who takes up all the charges on her shoulder is our madam."

"Oh, I didn't know this," Nikita said.

"We run behind love wishing to live our life like any other woman but it doesn't happen with us," Ishika said.

"Don't run behind love but be in love," Naina said, "I mean be always in love with God, with people, with animals, with plants."

Nikita's phone rang. Call from home. She went outside to talk freely.

"Why don't you go to your home and try if they take you back?" Saloni said.

"I tried but they are not even ready to talk with me. My dad has passed away. My step mother stays with her son at our house. They don't even want to talk to me," Ishika said.

"They are not supposed to do like this with you. That's your father's house," Saloni said.

"You are right but what can I do? Anyway," Ishika said, "Naina, can you please pass me the bottle of water? It is down beside the bed."

She passed the water bottle to Ishika. Ishika took out a miniature of ninety ml Royal Stag from her purse and said that her customer gave it to her last night. Mixing it with some water in a bottle, she drank it.

"I don't get to drink until my customers come and give me. Nowadays, I hardly have any jobs so barely I can drink," Ishika said.

"Madam," Suresh called from outside. "Vinay ji is calling both of you, go in room number seven."

"Oh, resting nicely, now customer has come. Why do they come in the afternoon?" Saloni was annoyed, "I don't like to work in the afternoon."

"Vinay ji didn't tell me to call you, Saloni madam," Suresh said.

"Okay, good." Saloni was relieved.

Ishika and Naina were walking towards the room. Ishika asked, "Suresh, why only we two? Where are the others?"

"Manager told me to call you both. You know girls are less in the afternoon. People who come from outside, they didn't reach yet."

"Hmmm, okay."

Naina's eyes forgot to blink as she entered the room. She was going to say something but her mouth could not utter a single word. She wanted to run away from the room but her feet got stuck to the floor.

Darshan was sitting on the bed, holding a beer can in his hand! He smiled looking at them.

Vinay ji introduced, "Meet Naina and Ishika."

Naina uttered a few words, "Vinay ji, I don't want to do this job."

"Why, what happened?"

"Nothing, I am going to the room."

"Okay, go."

Naina went back to Saloni's room and sat on the bed, trying to compose herself. Past good memories randomly flashed in her mind when Darshan, Sheena and she went for movies. They went to sea beaches together. They spent good times together when the brothel was closed due to police checking.

Ishika came to take her purse and mobile phone.

"Are you going to give him service?" Naina asked.

"Yes, I am going because I need money. You know I don't get too many jobs. So, I have to go, Naina. Why are you bothering? These people are like that. If I don't go and give him service, he will take some other girl in some other place. I will lose my job. You know how much hard work I do to make customers come to me. I give them massage, service and every possible thing they request for." Ishika got a little excited.

"Customers who come here to meet us, have wives at home as well," Naina said it not to Ishika but to herself to suppress the sudden overflowing emotion. It was hard to believe for her that Sheena just went home two weeks back and Darshan came here to sleep with someone else.

"Naina, I am going. If you want, you can call up Sheena and tell her Darshan had come,"

Ishika said. The ninety ml peg of Royal Stag that she just had sometimes back was doing its job.

"No Ishika, I don't want to talk about all this with her over the phone now, you may tell her,"

Naina said. Ishika took her purse and mobile phone and went off.

Closing her eyes, Saloni was listening to music in her mobile phone. She removed her earphones and got up on the bed. "What happened?" Saloni asked inquisitively. She might have sensed something went wrong.

Lowering her head, Naina was pressing her forehead. She looked up at Saloni. "Darshan came here as Sunil ji's customer!"

"What?" Saloni's mouth fell open.

"Sheena helped him with money from her savings for taking a new apartment. She used to pay his bill thinking she was saving his money. Poor girl dreaming Darshan would marry her!"

"I told so many times to Sheena, not to trust these people."

"You know Saloni, how is our situation here. You had been through the same. We all look for love, support and care in life. Sheena too was looking for that."

"Look Naina, I have told Sheena many times, Darshan is not good for her. He comes and meets her because it's fun for him. He was never serious in making a family with Sheena.

But she never listened to me," Saloni said.

Naina kept quiet. Saloni took out cigarettes and a lighter from her purse.

"Oh good, you both are here. I was looking for you two," Veena said as she entered the room.

Chapter 17

Veena was looking beautiful in a turquoise silk sari that had silver embroidery work all over. She had tucked white flowers in her hair. Her dazzling junk jewellery were adding extra beauty to her looks. At the workplace, she never did much make-up and all but that day she really did put extra effort on her looks it seemed.

Naina told her, "Madam, you are looking so beautiful. Is there something special tonight?"

She smiled beautifully making the room shine brighter. "My husband gifted this sari long back when we were together," she said.

"Wow! Is your husband coming to see you tonight?"

"We are going to visit God at the temple tonight. It's twelve hours journey from here. My husband will be coming there with his friends. We will meet each other after a very long time. He called up Sanjay and arranged this trip," Veena said. She was beaming.

"Really great. Happy for you," Saloni said.

Veena happily sat on the bed holding her sari carefully. Then she asked, "Do you both want to donate some money in the name of God?"

"Who all are going Madam with you?" Naina asked.

"From our building, Sanjay, Raju, Meena and I, Sailesh, Neelima, and few others from the nearby buildings are also joining us."

They gave her some money to be donated in the temple. Then Naina asked, "Madam, will you also feed bread to the starving people begging outside the temple?"

"Why do you want to feed beggars? I will give something if I can. There are so many peoplebegging outside the temple."

"Madam, beggars are human beings having the same soul within them that we have. They Are not different from us. They are made of the same five elements of which we are made of. We all are situated in the supreme consciousness, just we are not aware. They are begging food outside the temple; we are begging inside the temple. They are asking from us; we are asking from God. In my next birth, I may sit outside the temple and beg food because of what I might have done hundred lifetimes back."

"If we all have the same soul then why are they beggars, we are prostitutes, few are criminals and few are entrepreneur or something else?" Saloni asked.

"We are born with destiny because of our own past life karma. We face different challenges, situations and sufferings in life all due to our past life actions. All these identities what you are talking about, are only for this present life time based on our situation, naturenature, and action. In next life, our soul will change its costume, so identity will be different.

"Depending on our present life karma, our future life identity and destiny will be different. So, we should not remain attached with any of our identity. The quality of our nature makes us do action. So more than our identity, we should focus on the quality of our character to upgrade ourselves. Identities are always changing depending on our action and situation.

"There are three types of Karma. Prārabdha karma, Sanchit karma and Kriyaman karma. Prarabdha karma is what we go through in this life; it is like the final destiny we are born to face in this life. Prarabdha Karma is a part of Sanchit karma. Kriyamana karma is present karma that we are performing. We perform Kriyamana karma according to our nature. This Kriyamana karma or the Agami karma is again sowing the seeds for future.

"In 'Gita',,' Lord Krishna said to Arjuna that the warriors of the Kauravas were already killed, they were predestined to die in the war so Arjuna should not refrain from the war but to fulfil his duty of being a Kshatriya to fight for the right cause to save the dynasty to restore Dharma.

"All we need to do is to perform karma keeping Lord Krishna in mind. We should dedicate all our actions to him to remain free from the bondage of karma. We can worship Lord and engage ourselves in his devotional services with all our love and devotion at our home too.

Any action we perform to live in the material plain can be performed as a devotional service for him. God is everywhere with us, most importantly he is within us. To feel the bliss within, we need to raise our vibrations."

Madam said, "Naina, we are in the wrong path so we need to worship him more so that he becomes happy and blesses us."

"Lord Krishna is the eternal consciousness bliss, always happy. We need to be happy by knowing the truth and receiving his grace. We have to move towards light from the darkness.

Knowledge will make us happy.

"Nowadays, we engage ourselves in too much artificial and superficial worshipping for materialistic gain and make deals with God. If God gives us a job, we will donate a golden crown in his temple. And this is doing no good to us, it is not making us spiritual, it is making us narrow minded, superstitioussuperstitious, and greedy. To earn money for that golden crown to be donated we may do something unethical.

"That is the reason I was telling you to feed hungry people. By feeding them, we are directly serving the Supreme Lord. Soul within their body is part of the God. So, by serving human beings and animals, we are actually serving God. By serving the needy and underprivileged beings, we actually serve him. We are killing innocent animals in the name of sacrifice. The actual meaning of sacrifice is killing our materialistic selfish desires and be a devotee of God."

Saloni asked, "Where are you going Madam, which temple?"

"That is a great temple, that idol of God is another form of Lord Krishna."

"Hmmm. We are not able to see another form of Lord Krishna within living beings. We definitely need God's idol to pray in front of him, to surrender to him, to offer him ourvhomage and take his prasad.

"I have seen street dogs and cows eat garbage from dustbin on the road side and no one isbothered. We keep our eyes closed seeing those hungry homeless animals on the street. I have seen people to throw stones on hungry street dogs. Cow is the only animal which helped mankind to settle down besides the river banks from the ancient ages.

"Those days, cows were the only animal that provided milk to people as the main nourishing food, they helped in farming. They were used for transportation from one place to another place. People went from one place to another place on bullock carts. Cows remained the best friend of human beings since the earliest civilisation.

"Now also, we celebrate Diwali with kheer and sweets made from cow milk. We make sewai with cow milk and celebrate Eid. Starting from the morning milk, tea, coffee, butter, cheese, afternoon paneer and curd, ghee for making biriyani, butter milk, all the deserts like firni, sweets, gulabjamunGulab jamun, ice cream, etc. food products are made from cow milk.

"Their leather is being used to make our purse, shoes, beltbelt, and jackets. Their cow dung Is used as fuel to cook food in village area, their bones are used as fertilisers or bone mills. Cow is nourishing us with its milk from our childhood. Mostly all the baby food products are made from cow milk. Milk is our everyday food. We should be grateful to cows. And respect them for their selfless and generous contribution to the mankind."

"Naina, I just came to ask some money from you to be given to the God for your own benefit, so that you receive his grace and you are telling so many things to me," Veena said.

"Because I want you to understand, what actually needs to be dedicated to the God is our karma, not money. We human beings need money to survive in this material world but God is above Maya and we have to feel God with our unconditional love and devotion. We go in a temple and buy some sweets and flower and then dedicate them to God after standing in queue for hours and then visiting his idol for few seconds!

"Sometimes we can visit the idol soon by paying some money. More than paying attention to visit God's idol somehow, we should pay attention to our own action to elevate our consciousness. You just need to do your duty

, that's it. That's why Lord Krishna says in Gita, he who sees action in inaction, and inaction in action, is the most intelligent person. Then we don't need to rush to see his idol. We can feel him everywhere."

"Madam, tea." Badal came inside to serve tea.

They took the small still glasses of tea from the tray. Veena asked Badal, "Are Raju and Meena ready? Where is Sanjay?"

"Madam, they all are ready. They are also having tea. Your car will reach here any moment now, after having tea, you may go downstairs."

"Okay."

Saloni told, "Madam, I need to go to the parlour tomorrow. I have an appointment for hair straightening."

"What time will you go?" Veena said.

"I will go at three pm, will be back late in the evening. I will do pedicure and manicure too," Saloni said.

"Okay, go."

They were having tea silently until Badal's piercing scream made them shudder. "Everybody leave, quickly." Without wasting any minute, they were on the main road.

Chapter 18

All the females came outside on the road, making it crowded. Walking under the vast blue sky, breathing in the fresh air felt good compared with how they lived in a carton box like place that had artificial white light for all day and night, making it difficult to understand whether the time was morning or evening; whether the day was cloudy or rainy.

Naina was walking by one side of the road. Aarohi was with her. Manisha called them from a little far. They stopped walking and waited near the traffic signal. The loud horns of the cars and buses were piercing through their ears. "Shall we go to the beach? As he said, they may call us back within a few hours," Manisha said as she came near to them.

"Do you both want to go to one of my favourite place in Mumbai?' Naina asked.

"Sure, but where?"

"Mount Mary in Bandra. We will light some candles and come back."

"Okay, let's go."

A taxi dropped them at Mount Mary. Naina used to find this place very peaceful. She had come here countless times. Once, long time back, Naina and Sherya, after spending a whole night at a disco in Juhu got into an auto and told him to drop them at Mount Mary. It was around four-thirty am then. They both had a lot of tequila shots and vodka with orange juice.

After reaching there, they sat on the staircase, thinking after some time they would go back but they didn't realise how and when they fell asleep on the steps.

Morning's bright sunlight fell on Naina's closed eyes. She opened her eyes and found herself and Sherya on the steps of Mount Mary. They both were so astonished that they couldn't even talk for some time, thinking how they could sleep outside like that! Later, late in the morning they reached home.

***

Standing by the candle shop, Naina was thinking of her friends with whom she used to come there so many times. She thought of lighting some candles on behalf of them.

"The silence of this place is beautiful," Aarohi said, breaking the silence.

"Hmm, I have lots of memories of one of my very good friend with whom I used to come here almost every morning to light some candles. I hope he is fine wherever he is," Naina said.

"He was your boyfriend, right?" Manisha said.

"Yes, we were very much in love, deep love. That's a different story, will tell you some other day," Naina said.

In the candle shop, there were houses, couples, babies, etc. all made up of wax. Manisha and Aarohi got a home and a couple made of wax to offer to Mother Mary to get it returned by multiple times. Naina took a few candles.

"Let us go upstairs and light these."

The silence of the place had made them fall silent. Cool breeze was so refreshing. The sea could be seen from there. Slowly, the sky was becoming darker. They lit up the candles and closed their eyes.

***

They were walking along the beach, looking for a suitable place to sit. People were sitting in couples and in small groups, scattering here and there. Their hair and clothes were blowing in the wind. They sat on the wall facing towards the sea, looking at the continuous making and breaking of the waves; a view that was a treat to the eyes.

"How unpredictable is our life you see, we keep running around from one place to another place. Our life is like a traveller, walking on the path of life, running after a mirage. When our journey will come to an end God knows, maybe with our death," Manisha said.

"Our soul never dies; it continues its journey. For the soul, every death is a new beginning of a new journey. We think we die but we don't, we only change our gross body till our soul attains Moksha. This is the eternal truth," Naina said.

"When will we think of all this, our only motto in life is to earn money and fulfil the needs of our family," Aarohi said.

Manisha asked her, "Aarohi, you have completed graduation, right? Then why did you choose this profession?"

"I did my studies in Bengali and English was my second language, my dear," Aarohi said,

"Wherever I tried for job, everywhere people needed fluent English-speaking girls. Even if you want to marry; you need to be convent educated and fair looking. So, my plain graduation with my dark complexion was of no use for the job and marriage market. Once I got a job in a company but couldn't continue due to the office politics among the employees.

Later, I got a job in a cosmetic shop as a sales girl."

"Working as a sales girl was a better option than what you are doing now," Manisha said.

"What brought you here?"

Aarohi took a deep breath before she briefed her life story. "I was doing fine in life until I got married and gave birth to our first child, a girl. My husband and his family got depressed so much. They wanted a son. We tried next year but again, a girl was born. It's hard for you both to even imagine the amount of torture I went through.

"I used to do all the household work and got very little food. So many times, I had starved. I couldn't feed my babies. They were not getting nutrition and care. My husband used to beat me so much that I couldn't tolerate his torture. He used to beat me with stick, shoes, whatever was available.

"I left his house and came back to my father's house. We had a financial crisis at home. I joined the cosmetic shop again. My mother and sisters were looking after my daughters. I was so frustrated with torture and penury. My husband came to my father's house to meet me and there also, he used to shout at me.

"I wanted to give good healthy food, good education to my daughters and wanted to run away so that he couldn't find me. Someone in the cosmetic shop told me that I can earn good money in Mumbai. Then I came here to raise my children and give them a good life."

"Oh, you had suffered a lot," Manisha said.

"How big are your daughters now?" Naina said.

"Both are studying in a boarding school. The elder one is in class nine and the younger one is in class eight," Aarohi said.

"Wow! Grown up ladies they are. Just few more years of struggles and you will live a tension free life," Manisha said.

"I hope so." She smiled faintly.

"Why are you sounding so low?" Naina asked.

"You see the situation of our work is so bad nowadays. Customers look for new faces, new figures. They keep changing girls. To make a customer regularly come to me, I work so hard.

So many customers are asking to give service without condom."

"Yes, it happened with me too."

"Sometimes, I gave them service without condom because they were not able to ejaculate with the condom on. They were becoming tired, too tired but were not able to ejaculate.

They were frustrated to ejaculate somehow."

"Hmm."

"This happens when people are habituated to excessive masturbation. Then they can't ejaculate normally," Naina said, "It happens when people see too much of pornography. Then they keep thinking about those virtual seen in their mind and can't concentrate in the present moment when they are actually engaged in sex. So, they don't enjoy the real sex because they are habituated to see other people having sex, followed by masturbation."

"Pornography is not letting them enjoy the real sex by keeping their mind engaged in some imaginary world."

"Exactly, pornography encourages in masturbation and in illicit sex. Pornography is an addiction, which makes people frustrated by keeping them confined within the virtual world. Pornography influences them so much that they actually lose excitement while having real sex with a woman because they don't find any match in reality and what they have seen in the film. So, they keep changing woman in the hope of more excitement and later become more frustrated. Pornography encourages to peep in other's privacy. This can become so bad in the long run to get back in normal life."

"How innocently they ask sometimes, 'Do you do HIV test every month'?"

"What do you say then?"

"I say, I do HIV test in every three months." Manisha winked at them. "In reality, I didn't check for more than five years."

They broke into laughter.

Chapter 19

There were a few food joints nearby. Hawkers were selling ice creams, roasted corns, tea and coffee. Manisha got ice creams for all.

"Thanks Manisha, I simply love dark chocolate," Naina said.

"You are welcome, Naina."

Aarohi was quietly looking at the sea. Manisha asked her, "Aarohi, what are you thinking so much? Is there something that is bothering you?"

"I wonder sometimes when I think, people in our country worship different forms of feminine energy in the form of Goddesses, like Laxmi for wealth, Sarasvati for knowledge, Durga for overall well-being, Kali for power; then why the women are being raped, beaten, tortured, exploited?" Aarohi said.

"People have lost the feeling of love, respect, and empathy. Their consciousness is so low that their mentality is restricted within their basic sensual need and so they are selfish."

"People pray to Laxmi or Durga for material gain. So, they don't find any similarity between their daughter and Laxmi and between their wife and Durga. Goddess Laxmi will give wealth, daughter Laxmi will take away wealth during marriage. Wife Durga doesn't have weapons but **Godde**ss Durga is holding weapons, so it is safe to beat wife, they can't hit back," Manisha said.

"What do you think about symbolism in **Hindu**ism ? Why there are multiple forms of Gods and Goddesses?" Aarohi said.

"We worship deities and devatas in different forms because they rule different energies in **the** he universe. When we want to be connected with particular energy, we need blessings from them. Symbolism is necessary in our day-to-day life so that we can visualise them and worship. Visualisation is a part of meditation to be united with the divine. Symbols and idols of gods and goddesses make us feel more closely related with them.

"We feel more closely connected with them when we have their idols and when we read stories from Puranas and Shastras. Our prayer and worships to devatas and deities are a medium for us to feel connected with them and to get their blessings for living in a materialistic world. The supreme almighty is Lord Krishna. We worship him in so many forms as per our nature, wishes and desires which are perfectly alright.

"We worship gods and goddesses in particular forms; for example, the symbol of Durga has ten hands to hold different weapons to be well equipped. Her vehicle is lion-the strongest and most fierce animal of the jungle. The inner meaning is to fight against injustices with all your power, vigour, and dignity to kill evil, wrong and vice to restore Dharma.

"Durga is symbol of Shakti or the positive energy. Our consciousness is the Purusha or the Brahman. Now, if we take the weapons as spiritual consciousness, then spiritual consciousness and positive energy are merged to kill the demon which is our dark negative thoughts. This is a symbolism of Moksha or the Liberation.

"Again, the symbol of Kali is also energy. She is dark, naked, fierce, and holding a sword in one hand and a cut head on the other hand. She appears to cut ignorant and evil minds with her sword. The sword is similar to the spiritual consciousness. The cut head is similar to our false ego, which after being removed we are no more into illusion.

"Kali with her sword is the union of spiritual consciousness and energy. Spirituality begins with the cutting of false ego. Kali is widely worshipped in Tantra practise because Kali symbolises Moksha, Kundalini energy. Kundalini energy rises through the six chakras of the body to reach the crown or the sahasrara chakra.

"Kundalini energy is the most powerful spiritual positive energy, the most important vital force which is actually the energy of creation, our sexual energy. To awaken the Kundalini energy, our mind should be filled with unconditional love, compassion, and devotion, without any false ego. Kundalini yoga is not any kind of casual yoga practise. This is actually the toughest spiritual practise which unites one with the divine.

"People kill innocent animals in the name of sacrifice in front of Kali. Now think logically, Kali killed the evil demons to restore Dharma, why would she need an innocent animal's blood? This is our misconception and limitation. We need to cut our false ego to surrender ourselves to God.

"That is what sacrifices means, removing ignorance and evil with the weapon of knowledge. The symbol of Lord Shiva, that is all about sacrifice and being a yogi. His trident is a symbol of eternal consciousness bliss. Durga used this weapon to kill the demon," Naina said.

"Is Tantra practice a positive spiritual practice?" Aarohi said.

"Tantra simply means technique. To get enlightenment, people try to awaken the Kundalini energy. This awakening process is Tantra practise. In this process, we need techniques, mantras and yantras. Yantra means symbol. Meditation, pranayama, and the skilful handling of sexual energy comes under the tantra or the techniques.

"Mantra is the repeated chanting of God's name to hear them to attract the positive energy of the universe to inculcate positivity within us. Yantra is symbolic appearance of the God, which we visualise while doing meditation. When we combine these three into our regular spiritual practise, then it is Tantra Sadhana.

"But I tell you, love is the best Tantra practice ever. If your heart is filled with unconditional love for God and his creations that is the best Tantra practice one can ever do. Demigods and demi-goddesses sit on lotus flower or they have lotus flower in their hand. This lotus is a symbol of the win over negativity.

"Lotus blooms in stagnant muddy water. It takes its nutrition from the rotten muddy soiled water, means lotus being in a negative situation, converts the negativity into its positive nutrition and then blooms as a lotus. Lotus is the symbol of devotion and wisdom," Naina said.

"Let us go and have some coffee," Aarohi said.

Chapter 20

There was a tea, coffee, and cold drinks stall at the opposite side of the beach. They went there. There were pizza and other snacks inside the glass case.

"Do you want pizza?" Naina asked, looking at them.

"Oh yes," they said in unison.

Naina placed the order for pizza and coffee. They stood by the side of the tea stall.

Aarohi said, "When we talk about spirituality, then mind becomes calm. I liked the way you described the weapons as spiritual knowledge and how it is replacing ignorance from mind by cutting the head which symbolises false ego."

"Lord Krishna says in the 'Gita', to cut our ignorance with the weapon of knowledge,"

"I heard a beautiful story. I still remember," Aarohi said.

"Which story? Our Puranas have so many beautiful colourful learning stories

which have so much of morals and meaning in them."

"Once there was a churning of ocean between the gods and demons, for the immortal nectar of life. Lord Vishnu took the incarnation of a turtle to be the solid base on which the churning took place. First thing that came out from the churning was poison which was drunk by Lord Shiva. Later, the nectar came out.

"When the nectar was to be divided within the gods, one demon named Swarbhanu came in disguise to drink the nectar. But Sun and Moon recognised him and told to Lord Vishnu. Then Lord Vishnu had cut his head with his Sudarshan Chakra. The head was named Rahu and the body was named Ketu. That is why Rahu eclipses the Sun and Moon."

Naina smiled. "Beautiful story, this story is one of the best symbolic expressions of our character building and career building through the knowledge of spirituality. This story holds high importance in astrology too. The poison which came out first is similar to our impurities,

darkness and negativity which come under Tamasik qualities, the quality of ignorance.

"Lord Shiva is the god of Tamasik qualities. Lord Shiva swallowed all the ignorance by drinking the poison. It means overcoming and transforming the negativities such as greed, envy, fear, hatred, anger, and false ego present in our mind. These are our mental blockages unless we overcome these hatreds and negative feelings, we will not get the nectar. The poison can be cleared by establishing love in mind.

"Finally, the nectar came out. Here, nectar is symbolising the spiritual consciousness, meaning we understand that we are 'Jiva' having immortal soul within heart. The turtle at the base symbolises the stability of the mind.

Swarbhanu was a demon whose head symbolises false ego which was cut off by Sudarshan Chakra, the weapon of spiritual consciousness.

"The body part is Ketu, which doesn't have any false ego. The remaining body Ketu symbolises our quality of nature. Once the false ego is cut, then the body will no more be an illusion. That is why Ketu is the most spiritual of all nine planets in astrology because it doesn't have false ego and it's detached from illusion.

"Ketu removes illusion and it is the planet of detachment and Moksha. Though Rahu and Ketu are not real planets having physical body. They are shadow planets, nodes of the moon, calculated point. Rahu is the most cunning illusionary planet. It doesn't have its nature attached with it. So, it generally behaves like the planet it is conjunct with or as its depositor.

"Rahu generally amplifies the quality of the conjunct planet and the sign in which it sits. It is the never-ending desire. Rahu and Ketu are the most karmic planets for which we take birth again, and again. Rahu is our present life karma, which is to be performed in this life. Ketu is our past life acquired knowledge and character, which helps us in this life to perform karma.

"Rahu drank the nectar but could not digest. So, it is never ending desire. We take birth for fulfilling our desire. The house and sign where Ketu sits in the horoscope that is our actual nature because Ketu couldn't drink the nectar so Ketu represent our past and real nature.

"The nakshatra on which Ketu sits, tells a lot about our nature. Rahu is desire, cunningness and illusion. Our horoscope is just the snapshot of our past life karma to be executed in this life time. Which karma of our past life will fructify at what time, that can be seen through the mahadasha system.

"As you said, Rahu eclipses Sun and Moon, it is true. If Rahu sits with sun in close conjunction in the horoscope, then past life karma is associated with name, fame and authority which we will be in difficulties in this life time. Eclipse means covering the light, shadowing the light. But eclipse doesn't last longer.

"Later, Rahu amplifies the qualities of sun. Rahu and Ketu are our desire and character. Rahu and Ketu are coiled serpents, which symbolises Kundalini energy for spirituality. That is why those houses are very important in which house, nakshatra and sign Rahu and Ketu are placed in the horoscope.

"Things happen in our life depending mainly on the Mahadasha and Antardasha of planets and their Nakshatras and Nakshatra lords) that we go through. We all have our ascendant; we all are born with a particular ascendant. Ascendant is the most important deciding factor of our horoscope because the whole chart is made depending on the ascendant position.

"We will have qualities and characteristics within us according to our ascendant and ascendant lord, moon sign lord and sun sign lord. If there is a cluster of planets in any sign, that sign and the sign lord will dominate the qualities and characters in us.

Moon in Astrology represents our mind. Moon is very much important planet in our life after the ascendant lord because if our mind doesn't work properly, we can't perform any action.

"The house and the sign, where moon is placed in horoscope, show the direction and state of mind. The nakshatras on which the planets are posited at the horoscope are most important to study our karma in minute details. Sun signifies our soul," Naina said.

They were sitting on the chairs near the coffee stall. A little boy was serving pizza to them.

Naina looked at the boy. His age was around ten or eleven. Manisha also noticed him. She said, "How sad, these small little boys should be studying and playing but they are working at shops."

Aarohi said, "Our children could have been in his place if we wouldn't have been doing prostitution. At least our children are not facing so much of struggles in life because we are facing it. I don't know what will happen later. But I have tried to do whatever I could."

After the pizza, they had coffee. Naina asked them, "Shall we sit on the beach again?"

Manisha said, "Sure. It is nine pm only."

Aarohi said, "People use astrology as a tool of predicting events only. We believe that Astrology can change luck by wearing stones and doing remedies or by giving donation. Now you are saying horoscope is the map of the journey of our soul, how do you explain it?"

"Astrology is not only a predictive tool; it is the gateway of spiritual knowledge. Astrology helps us to know our real self and the journey of our soul. Our birth chart or the horoscope is divided into four parts. They are dharma triangle, money triangle, desire triangle and the Moksha triangle.

"To move forward in the path of Moksha, we need to overcome the money and desire triangle. Also, we can say, money must be earned traversing through the path of dharma.

After fulfilment of desires on the path of Dharma, we can move towards the path of Moksha. That is why, first comes Dharma, followed by money, desire and Moksha triangle.

"Dharma triangle represents our family lineage, guru, luck , higher knowledge ,faiths and beliefs. First, fifth and ninth house makes Dharma triangle. First house is our ascendant; we, our intelligence and physical body. You can count anticlockwise from the first house to reach the fifth house, which is the house of love, romance, creativity, and children.

"Then you again count anticlockwise and reach in the ninth house . in the basic kalpurush chart, Aris, Leo, and Sagittarius signs fall on these signs. These are fire signs. Fire sign represents dharma, creativity, inspiration, leadership.

"Same way second, sixth and tenth house make money triangle. Second house is of our values, family, wealth, etc. Sixth house is enemy, disease, loan, etc. Tenth house is mainly our profession, name, fame, etc. These three houses are the money triangle showing the path nature of your income.

"Third, seventh and eleventh house make desire triangle. This triangle shows our desire, wish fulfilment and gain in this life. Eleventh house denotes wish fulfilment and gain. These houses and signs show the way to fulfil your desire before getting Moksha.

"Fourth, eighth and twelfth house make Moksha triangle. In the basic Kalpurusha chart, the sign falls in those houses are Cancer, Scorpio and Pieces which are watery signs. Water represents intuition, intensity, nurturing, emotion, empathy. Ascendant, sun, or moon in these signs make a person emotional and intuitive.

"Based on your ascendant, you have to see where the signs of dharma, artha, karma and Moksha of kalpurush kundli are falling in which houses of your chart. Then you divide your own horoscope in four parts and find out which triangle is strong in your chart.

"For example, if your artha triangle is strong but the signs fall in those houses are dharma signs according to the kalpurush chart, then you will earn money in the path of dharma. You can take your own horoscope and analyse your own journey. The divisional charts and nakshatras help us know about our karma in minute details. Nakshatras are most important to study. Mahadasha and Antardasha lord's nakshatra and their lords can cause big changes at their dasha or antardasha."

"In the newspapers or magazines, I see prediction based on the zodiac sign. Is that zodiac

sign my ascendant?" Manisha asked.

"No, that is not our ascendant sign. Our ascendant sign is the rising sign in the east when we take birth. Ascendant lord is like the sun of a chart that illuminates the whole chart. Ascendant sign changes in every two hours. To know the ascendant sign, you need to have your exact birth date, timetime, and place. Birth chart or the horoscope is made based on that."

"How do we see our journey in the horoscope?" Aarohi asked.

"The first thing you need to see is ascendant and its lord, Moon, and the Sun. See their house, sign, lordships, nakshatra lords, placements, and conjunctions. The sign, sign lord and nakshatra lord of moon tells a lot about you. Then you see what the mahadasha was running during your birth Mahadasha **of planets starts based on Moon's nakshatra.**

"See where that mahadasha planet is sitting, in which sign and in which nakshatra. That tells a lot about your nature. In the mahadasha or antardasha of that planet, you may go through big changes.

"Then you see the placement of Mars, Jupiter, Saturn, and other planets. See where, in which sign and in which nakshatra your Rahu and Ketu is placed. Study the nakshatras,

conjunction, lordship and aspects, sign, and house placement of each planet. Each house and eachplanet have so much meaning in them. Each nakshatra has a story and that story is important to know. These are the basic factors.

"Then to know about your present condition, you see which mahadasha you are going through at present. This mahadasha lord is your guide for these few years. You will go through different situation depending on the mahadasha of the planet you are running through. Mahadasha lord defines the type of people we meet in that particular planetary period and the nature of our karma depending upon the nakshatra on which the mahadasha lord is sitting. Then you see that nakshatra lord's position. Nakshatra lord of the mahadasha planet is very important to study. Thus, mahadasha lord prepares you and takes you ahead in the journey of your soul. See the nakshatra, house, sign, lordships, conjunctions, and aspect of mahadasha planet and antardasha planet.

"Mahadasha lord will put us in a situation depending on his current transiting house. Thetransit of current mahadasha planet is most important for anything to happen in life along with the antardasha planet transit. The transits of the planets happen in mathematical calculative manner.

"And you must see the transit of planets from your ascendant to understand your present situation. Here you should not get confused by seeing a transit from Moon because all the physical manifestation takes place from the ascendant position. Even if you run through your Sade sati (Saturn's seven and half years transit before, over and after Moon), still mahadasha Lord, antardasha lord and their nakshatra lord is the most important.

"Things will manifest physically as per your dasha lord and as per their transit. Here desh, kaal and patra concept (place, time and individual) is very important because you have to understand your situation based on your surroundings and upbringing and your own situation.

To know or understand every day's incidents or triggering of an incident you have to see moon's transit in each house and interaction with planets. Moon's transit in house will give the result or trigger some incidents as per the house through which moon is transiting that very day. Moon 's interaction while transiting over planet and if the dasha of that planet is running, then things will happen as per the planet is supposed to give result.

For example, if the moon transits your tenth house and any planet is sitting on the tenth house. Moon's transit in that house will activate or trigger some incident regarding your profession or carrier. Another example, when planets mostly transiting in your second, seventh or eleventh house, specially Jupiter or Venus , along with that when moon will cross these planets in those houses and you go through the dasha of those planets transiting in those houses, it may trigger some incidents or activate something regarding your marriage.

Once you understand moon's everyday transit and how it making things happen, you understand the beauty of Astrology. This moon's transit triggers any event in day to day basis depending upon your Dasha lord planet and the promises according to your horoscope.

"If any of your planet is in Gandanta and its mahadasha or antardasha has started, then you may have to face difficulties and through the difficulties you will learn and grow. Gandanta is a Karmic knot that gives some sufferings.

"You may not attend all the nine planetary periods in this life. You will go through the remaining balance mahadasha in your next lives. After death, soul may stay in subtle body in the atmosphere for many years depending upon the karma. Later, it may take birth into a gross body when the mahadasha planetary period starts for that soul to act in the material

plain," Naina had to stop as Aarohi's phone rang.

Sharma was calling. Aarohi answered the call.

***

"We were having a good time on the sea beach,beach; I wish we could be there for some more time," Manisha said in the taxi.

"Huh, we had spent a beautiful evening there," Aarohi said, "Naina, thanks to you for sharing your astrological knowledge. From past few months, I am listening to spiritual mantra chanting and videos on YouTube. It keeps me calm and peaceful from within."

"But how did you learn astrology, Naina?" Manisha wanted to know.

"I am learning from Google and YouTube and **observing my own life. It** is such a vast subject. Astrology is called Jyotish, the light of God."

"Astrology is really interesting."

"Astrology is being misused nowadays. Either we are stuck within gemstones and remedies or we make fun of astrologers and astrology. Or we look only for the monthly and weekly predictions. We should study astrology to evolve ourselves," Naina said.

"According to your explanation, our life is predestined and we are not free to choose. So, whether we commit sins or we remain ignorant, that is there in our karma," Aarohi said.

"Yes, whether we remain ignorant or we get enlightened that is already predestined and things will happen as they are supposed to happen, depending on planetary transit and your planetary period. That is how universe works mathematically.

"You are now listening to me because the planetary mahadasha of your ninth lord or planet sitting in ninth house or the mahadasha or antardasha of Ketu or Jupiter must be going on.

Maybe your mahadasha lord planet is sitting on a nakshatra, which is very good for spirituality. So, you picked up interest in watching spiritual videos.

"There may be some conjunction in your birth chart that is good for spirituality and the mahadasha of that conjunct planet has started now. So, you are getting interest in spirituality. It will make you work in that direction.

"Even the planets have Satvik, Rajasik and Tamasik qualities. Jupiter, SunSun, and Moon have Satvik qualities. Venus and Mercury have Rajasik qualities. Rahu, Ketu, Saturn, and Mars have Tamasik qualities. Planets control us and put us into different situation according to their own nature and character.

"For example, Jupiter, Moon, Mercury, and Venus are natural beneficial planets. They are natural beneficial but depending on their lordships and position in a particular horoscope, they may give us less beneficial, neutralneutral, or malefic results.

"Saturn, Mars, Rahu, and Ketu are natural malefic but depending on their position in our birth chart, they may give good results. They are called malefic planets because we face hardship, struggle and downfall in their planetary periods. But through that we learn. They may take you to the highest of your carrier and status during their planetary mahadasha but with difficulties and hard work.

"Depending on their position in your chart, they may even stay neutral. So, you may not face any drastic challenges during the periods of those planets. So, we all are performing our own action as per our nature being guided by the ruling planets."

"Naina, we see sometimes babies are born blind. Within few years of birth, a baby becomes handicapped. Sometimes just after the baby takes birth, the parents die. What Karma that baby has done?" Aarohi asked.

"It is the past life remaining mahadasha and karma getting fructified in this life. May the age of the baby is two or five but actually the age of the soul is million years. It is the infinite soul which is constantly changing its outer shell or the gross body from life after life. This body is getting recycled from so many millions of past life times under the mahadasha and transition of planets.

"So, at the age of five, the baby was gone blind because the soul had to go through the situation of blindness at that particular time due to some past life karma. The knowledge of astrology helps us to understand our life situation better; it is not to scare us or to change our luck. Knowledge removes ignorance and makes us free from the unnecessary worries of life. Knowledge brings peace."

Chapter 21

The whole building and adjacent area was dark and quiet. Other days, the managers used to stand and wait for customers outside. But that night, only one or two people were standing in the far away distance. Building's gate was locked. Badal was standing near the gate with a bunch of keys. He opened the gate and they stepped inside.

The big lights of the lounge were switched off. Only one small light was shining in the corner. There was a dim light in the corridor too. Unlike the other busy evening, that night the place was very quiet. No one was laughing loud or talking over the phone. Everything was silent. They went inside. Saloni, Sophia, Ishika, Aarti, Jeni, Simran and Nafisa were sitting inside. Raju was making tea.

"Only you people? Where have the rest of the girls gone?" Manisha enquired.

"Few are busy and rest of the girls went home. Local Police informed to keep fewer girls," Aarti said.

"Oh, okay."

Vinay came in the hall. "Where is Tina?" He asked.

"Tina is busy," Raju told looking at the register copy of time and room number.

"When will she be free?"

"She just went ten minutes back."

Vinay looked at the females available and mumbled, "Whom to give, whom to give?"

"What are you thinking so much, whom to give?" Jeni enquired.

"Pranav has come, he wants Tina," Vinay said.

Pranav was a very rich man. He used to come two to three times or more every week and stayed the whole night. Every hour or two, he used to change women. But most of the time, Tina used to be with him. Pranav was soft-spoken, well-behaved person. He used to give good tips to all the women. He liked to talk and gossip a lot. He never drank alcohol and never smoked cigarette.

Jeni said, "I can go, I will keep him busy till Tina is free. Then you can send Tina."

"Jeni, don't let him ejaculate. If he ejaculates, he will leave immediately," Vinay instructed.

Jeni smiled wickedly. "I know Vinay ji. I will talk with him for some time and then I will give service. Again, I will talk and then little service; like that I will keep him engaged and the time will pass."

"Good. Then you go. Whom will you take with you now?"

"He likes young girls, so I can take Aarti now."

"Okay then Aarti and Jeni, you both go. I am going to collect the payment. Give good service,"

Vinay said and he looked at the corner. "What happened to Ishika? Why is she crying?" Vinay asked, looking at Nafisa.

They looked at the corner side near the small room where Ishika was sitting. Her tear drops were rolling down from her eyes, running down her cheeks; she was silent. Vinay went near her and said, "What happened to you? Did you drink too much in the evening?"

Ishika didn't reply anything. Vinay said, "Nafisa, come here. Give her water, talk to her. I have to go."

Nafisa said, "Ishika is still silent. Sometimes Manisha drinks too much, that night she will definitely do some drama."

"Oh! Look at you. What happened that night when you and Anita were totally drunk and out of control? You both were not ready to go to sleep only. Once, I was consoling Anita and once, I was consoling you. No one was ready to stop. Anita was going on telling, 'go from here, go from here'..' I was asking, whom was she telling to go but what would she reply, would she cry or talk?"

Nafisa went near Ishika. Sitting beside her, she placed her hand over Ishika's shoulder and wiped her tears with her other hand with a tissue. Manisha started laughing loudly. She said, "Really, it was so funny. Later in the afternoon, I had such a bad headache."

"Naturally, when you drink, you don't stop in two or three pegs," Sofia said.

"Saloni does the best thing after ,drinking; she takes class of everybody. No one is spared when she drinks too much," Aarohi said.

Monica came in the hall. She said, "You know what happened with Jasmine?" There was something in her voice, everybody looked towards her eagerly wanting to know what happened to Jasmine.

"What happened? Where is she?"

"She is in her room, crying. Her son has sold the small land she just bought a few months ago," Monica said.

Nafisa got up immediately. "Let's go and see."

Simran, Sofia, Ishika, and Naina went with her to Jasmine's room. Jasmine was aged.

She used to get fewer customers these days. When she came here for the first time, she came with a pimp who took away most of her money in the first few years, when her income was very good. She had a son and a daughter in her village.

Her husband didn't take care of Jasmine and her children. Moreover, her husband didn't take care of his own parents. He used to roam around here and there. He left home one day, leaving a note on the bed, 'I am going to take renunciation; I am going in search of God. **God** is calling me'..'

Jasmine didn't know what to do and how to run the family of six people. Later, she came Into prostitution. She loved a customer here, thinking he would marry her. That customer took Jasmine out from this place of course, but kept her only for three years with him and later, he left her. Then she came back to Sanjay's place again. Somehow, she bought little land in her village to make a small house there for the future. That was her only asset.

Jasmine was drinking some whisky mixed in water in a plastic bottle. Seeing them, she brokev into tears. Nafisa embraced her. "My son sold out the only saving of my life," Jasmine said, still sobbing, "I bought the land with so many difficulties." Sofia patted her arms.

"I gave so hard service, Sofia you know," Jasmine said, wiping her tears with a tissue, "I have even attended fourteen to fifteen customers in a single day. I didn't buy a new dress for me for months, saving money. I didn't eat any evening snacks. How I saved every single penny those days and my son sold it."

Naina was searching for words. What to say her, how to console her? What should she say about Maya, karmakarma, or the astrology here? How to explain to her and in which words?

She kept quiet. Raju called them, "Madams, go to the hall, Sharma ji is calling to all of you."

Nafisa said, "Get up Jasmine, don't cry. We have to go in the hall room, customer has come."

Jasmine stopped weeping. She wiped her face with a fresh napkin and applied some powder on face. Then she applied some lipstick on her lips. "Let's go," she said, "I will have to send money to my daughter next week."

They reached the hall and lined up themselves. Four people were sitting. Two of them were talking within themselves. They were aged around forty-five years or more. Other two were much younger than them in their late twenties or early thirties. One of the middle-aged man who was sitting at the corner, said, "Sharma, I am not choosing, you give me someone with the best service. I need good body massage; I am so tired tonight."

"Sir, you take Jasmine, the one standing at fifth from this side, in green colour sari. Best body massage and any kind of service you like, she will provide."

"Oh really, okay!" He agreed, looking at Jasmine.

"Jasmine, you go inside," Sharma said.

The next customer said, "Give me someone like her."

"Okay sir, you go with Ishika, the lady in golden lehenga choli."

He looked at Ishika. "Oh, this lady, she is Ishika!" He said, "I have heard a lot about her from my friend. I would love to go with her." He smiled.

One of the two people left asked, looking at Naina, "What is your name?"

She said, "Naina."

"Nice name." He smiled, "Naina, would you like to drink some whiskey with me?" She nodded her head smilingly. He then looked at Sharma, "Send her in the room."

The last one selected was Sofia. They came back in the inside hall.

"Good, no? Jasmine and Ishika both got jobs," Simran said as she sat on a bench.

"Hmm, I can have some more whiskey," Ishika said.

Chapter 22

The young man was sitting on the bed. There was a full bottle of Johnnie Walker Black Level twelve years, kept on the side table.

"Nice to meet you Naina, please sit," he said as he shook hands with her. "Do you like to drink or you simply agreed to give me company?"

She smiled. "I actually like to drink."

"Then we will enjoy the drink, right?"

"Of course."

"You can call me Jatin, I am from Surat," he added, "The city of diamonds."

"And textiles," Naina added.

Glasses were kept on the side table. She took two glasses and made the drink. They clanged glasses. Knocking on the door, Chintu entered with room service. Keeping the things on the bed, he asked, "Do you need anything, sir?"

"Can you get cheese balls, crispy potato fries and ice, please?

"Okay, sir. Please give me money for the room service."

He took out his purse from his pocket and gave a two thousand rupee note asking him to get change.

"Two minutes sir, I am just coming."

After Chintu left the room, Jatin told her, "I want to use your wash room. Please give the boy some tips when he gets back with the balance."

"Sure. Thanks, on his behalf."

Chintu came with ice and change within minutes. He told, he had ordered for the snacks. It would be there within fifteen minutes. Naina gave him money. He went happily.

"Why the lights are off in the hall room?" Jatin asked after taking a sip from his drink.

"There was some problem of police in the evening; though they have settled the problem,

Still it's better to be cautious. So, the lights are off and the gate is closed," Naina said.

"Don't you all get scared to work in such a situation?"

"Yes, we get scared but what to do? If we sit at home, what the people of our family will eat?"

"I salute you people; you sacrifice so much for your family."

Naina smiled a little. "Though our families are getting food and shelter but they are lacking education and morality. The children are growing up without proper culture because the mother is not at home and mostly, the father doesn't work. So basically, society is producing and growing ignorant people more."

"Naina, you came here to fulfil your basic needs but think of those who have lots of wealth but no education and good culture in the family. Look at me, my parents are rich business people, both were busy in their own work. I grew up almost without their love, care and guidance."

"Your father was busy but what about your mother? Was she busy too?" Naina said.

"My mother was very active in her social circle for social works. She was busy too. I have one brother and one more sister."

"Then who looked after you three brothers and sisters?"

"Domestic help and governess. We were lacking love and affection from our parents but had lot of fun in school days. I had a lot of friends. When you don't get love and affection at home, then you look for the same outside. The only thing I hated the most was to study. So many subjects, so many books and frequent exams."

Naina nodded her head. She said, "You just gather lots of knowledge and information and memorise them only to score good marks in the exams. You are not learning because you want to learn and know something. You are learning to compete in the class. This process of learning is not helping people to evolve.

"They are not learning or getting spiritual knowledge, so this education is not helping them to grow from within. After you complete your studies, you go and join any company, you'll find huge difference between what you've studied all the years and what you get to do at your work place.

"There is no scope to encourage and enhance your learning process, there is no scope for research and development. Unnecessarily, you had to memorise extra subjects. So, it did put pressure on your mind, which did not help you in exploring your real talents.

"When you are pressurised by the fear of exams and burdened with so much information and knowledge, you often cannot focus in studies. Worries and fear works within mind and then mind wants fun and relief outside studies. So, you mix up more with friends, play more games and avoid studies.

"The continuous pressure of memorising so much information, books, exams, competition and above all, the scolding and shouting of parents makes the mind so stressed that kids may not like to study at all. The kids who are intelligent in other things, they may not like to memorise this information at all. It depends a lot on the teacher to get your interest in

studies though."

Jatin said, "The main aim of our modern education is to get a job and a well settled life."

"True. This is the reason we are not evolving. You are lucky if you get a good teacher who makes you like your studies. Otherwise, the most interesting subject may be boring for you. It depends a lot on a teacher to discover and increase your interest in studies," Naina said.

Chintu knocked on the door. He had got the snacks.

"Good, the snacks came at the right time," Jatin said as he took a cheese ball.

"It's good Naina, try it," Jatin said.

She too had one. Medium sized boiled potato ball, fresh salty cheese inside was melting in the mouth.

After having a cheese ball, Naina asked, "How do you spend your time when you are not at office?"

"Mostly with my friends, games, drinks and party. Often, we go to some clubs or resorts, do party there and then again back to work."

"Don't you enjoy your work?"

"Enjoying work? How is that possible? I work because I have to work. If I don't work, how will I spend money?"

"So, you work only to earn money?"

"Yes, I work only to earn money and spend it as I wish. I don't think people work for anything else other than earning money."

"We all need money but money should not be our primary focus in life. Our duty, values, morals and ethics should be our priority. Then money comes secondary. When you perform work as your duty and you like what you do, money will naturally follow.

"But when you run after money then you take wrong decision. You tell lies, cheat or manipulate people because your main aim becomes to earn money somehow. Thus, you actually lose money in the long run as well as mental peace and self-respect.

"When you enjoy your work, you increase your potential. You like what you do, so you don't feel stressed. You feel fulfilled and engaged, so you don't need alcohol or girls to take away your stress. Your work then becomes your relaxation.

"Now you are working for money with stress and pressure, so you remove your stress by drinking, partying, enjoying illicit sex, etc. Thus, you lose your money and again run after money. But when you are truly engaged and involved in your work, then you feel happy within. You may drink alcohol or may go to party but that too very less.

"When you are happy from within, you are not stressed then you can be more productive and creative at your work. What I have seen here and discussed with people; I have found most of them are looking for joy outside their family. They are searching for pleasure outside their work. Kids are searching for joy outside of their own studies.

"The reason is they are not happy within their own work, own family, and own studies. Thus, in search of pleasure people are indulging more into wrong activities. You know why we search for joy outside our work because we think that our work is stressful. So, everything is becoming hectic for us, be it study or work. What do you think, what is lacking?" Naina asked.

"Right awareness is lacking," Jatin said, "Actually, you are correct, Naina. I couldn't study the subjects I liked because I had to join my father's business. My favourite subjects were s science but I had to study management. I never liked management subjects. My parents never valued my wishes and dreams. So, I feel comfortable with my friends. I have a lot of work pressure too. So, I try to spend a good time when I am free."

"How long does that good time last?"

"Few hours or few days maybe, I never thought of it that way. I work like a machine and then party harder."

"You should not work like a machine; it doesn't make you creative. It gives stress. You should enjoy your work and then naturally you work harder than enjoying party because you like what you do. Girls drink here because they try to cope up with the situation.

"In reality, your creativity and productivity are becoming less at work because you don't like what you do. If from your school days, you could have studied few selected subjects of your own choice along with spiritual knowledge, then you could have worked on those subjects only and become happy in life.

"Spiritual education is a must from childhood for the right upbringing, charactercharacter, and career building and right guidance in life. Without spiritual knowledge, we actually remainignorant."

His phone started ringing. "One-minute Naina, I have to take this call."

"Sure."

Chapter 23

"I lost this bet," Jatin said impatiently as he slid his phone on the side table.

"Do you regularly bet in cricket matches?" Naina asked.

"Yes."

He took some crispy potatoes from the plate. Naina too was chewing potato fries quietly.

"Are you upset for losing the match? Do you win most of the time?" Naina asked after some time.

With a broad smile on his face, he said, "No, I lose most of the time. I mainly enjoy the excitements. In such cricket betting, the actual gainer is the broker."

"Oh, really?"

"He can manage his five mobile phones at a time."

"Is it so?"

"Yes, calls keep coming in all the phones simultaneously and he picks up all the calls while writing the bets," he said with a smile on his face.

"Good to see you smile," Naina said.

"What's the big deal? I may win the next match."

"What! Then how will you stop this?"

"But why will I stop this? I like the excitement of match and make money as well, while having fun."

"When you make money by gambling, you don't have any respect for the earned money. You take it as a part of game and develop a tendency to spend money loosely for anything that you think will give you pleasure. Earning money by gambling will make your brain dull and will keep your thought process limited within the sensual objects."

"It will make my brain dull? What do you mean?"

"I mean, you will not be able to find greater purpose for living. The evolution and growth will stop. Your brain will remain engaged in gambling ideas. I see so many customers who come here, they love cricket betting. It has become like a popular culture. You never think this is wrong. You play it for money and fun.

"This becomes an addiction and never lets you be in peace. Either you are excited for winning or you are sad for losing. Once the excitement is gone, you look for it again. There is no peace in mind. You are just always running after pleasure and excitement."

"I get happiness in these things. I work so hard, then spend money in betting and partying. It makes me happy."

"Jatin, what you think is happiness, it is not. You think these things give you happiness, no. these things keep you in illusion. Our real happiness is in God. Our real happiness is in love. Spirituality makes you really peaceful and happy from within.

"You become truly happy when you live for higher purpose of life, you become happy when you get in touch with spiritual people and enquire about God. You feel really happy within when you serve humanity. That is the everlasting real happiness in life."

"My friends will laugh at me if I start to enquire about God and meet spiritual people. They will make fun of me. They say spirituality is for old people," Jatin said.

"Then find him within you. Start enquiring everything about yourself and search for your purpose in life. Self realisation is the best realisation. You don't need to go anywhere, Look within. You are not realising that you are already making fun of your own life. You are the most capable of doing things at your young age and you are wasting that age into drinking and partying other than doing something positive and constructive for your own as well as forvthe well-being of the society.

"Later in your old age, you will search spirituality in some pilgrimage and will make the holy place crowded and dirty with plastics and other garbage. You should make proper use of your energy other than wasting it for no good reason. Spiritual knowledge bestows love, peace and success in life."

"But I cannot imagine my life without these things."

"You are still a young boy who craves for chocolates. The process of growing is slow and gradual, it takes time and patience. The joy that removes fears and anxieties, is bliss. Obviously, you can't feel blissful by attaching your mind into small things which gives you worries."

"Hmm."

"Let me ask you one thing. You are a Krishna devotee, right? Do you follow what he says?"

"What does he say? I mean, I don't know what he says. We have his beautiful idol at home; we worship him, decorate him with lots of beautiful silk clothes, gold, and diamond jewellery.

We offer homage to him and take prasad," Jatin said.

"That is really great. What you do for him, they are like token of love for him. But while worshipping, you should also follow his instructions. Only worshipping without following his teachings isare not correct. The real worship of Lord Krishna is when you follow what he says.

Would you like your employees just to respect you as their boss or you would want them to follow your instructions as well?"

"What does he say? And how do you know about it?"

"Have you heard a book named 'Gita'?"

"I have seen in Hindi movies ,sometimes; in the court room a person takes oath keeping his hand on 'Gita' to tell the truth and then he lies."

"Exactly, I am talking about that book. People even donate 'Gita' after someone dies in the family. Though I don't understand what is the purpose of donating 'Gita' after death if the person didn't read it to remove his ignorance while living."

"My friends will laugh at me if I start reading 'Gita'."

"Why are you so afraid of the fools who laugh at anything they don't know? Without knowing and enquiring, they are confident about their own views and they even laugh. So, what can be a better example of foolishness than this? You should read 'Gita' for knowing and understanding yourself.

"Once you understand spirituality, then you will have sympathy for them. It may seem difficult to understand 'Gita' in the beginning but when you **enquire within and try to find answers, you will understand.**

"Lord Krishna loves everyone; we all can get his love and mercy. He is full of love and mercy. We can remove our delusion and be enlightened by the Lord's grace. He is there in everybody's heart but we don't know, so we search for him in the temples and pilgrimages.

"I believe, a pilgrimage is a clean mind which is free from greed, jealousy, hatred, anger, pride. Where there is humanity that is a holy place. In a pilgrimage, you will see business of flowers, coconuts, guest house, priests, God's idol, photo frame, sweets, etc. to earn money anyhow and all the hungry, helpless people begging just outside a temple. In some pilgrimages, you pay money and can visit the idol of the God with a VIP pass sooner than others.

"Money is a necessity, of course but there should be devotion, truthfulness, and honesty. The pilgrimages have become too much congested and polluted like our mind, full of negativities with lies, selfishness, lust, greed and envy. You can make your own place holy by being a devotee of the Lord and keeping the screen of your own mind clean. Giving donations, and taking responsibility **by spreading awareness,** makes you a better person each day."

Jatin nodded his head.

"You know Jatin," Naina said, "There are so many other examples of not taking responsibilities. Tonight, there was a woman named Jasmine, you must have seen her, she was standing in the queue with us, your friend went with her in the room."

"They are not my friends, our buyers. Whenever they come to my office, I need to bring them here every time. They spend time with the girls inside the room and I drink outside while waiting for them. Tonight, I thought of spending some time with you. I thought you may give me good company in drinking."

"I understood that you are a good person when you told me to give the service boy some tips, people generally give tips to the girls for giving good service or being compassionate."

Jatin smiled a little. "What were you telling that time? What happened to Jasmine?" Jatin asked.

"Her husband left her with two children and went somewhere in search of God, leaving behind people to starve."

"He didn't want to take responsibilities, I guess."

"Exactly, more than love or devotion for God, it is running away from responsibilities. There are yogis who leave their family life and take renunciation. They leave home for a much higher cause. Sometimes, people leave home and take renunciation to attain Moksha. They think by sacrificing the daily life action, Moksha can be attained.

"Sacrificing action doesn't mean not to work or to stop daily life action. Eating, breathing, thinking, meditating, etc. everything is action. You cannot stop working for even a single moment. But yes, the more peaceful you are, the more you are on the path of Moksha.

"You too can live like a yogi being with friends and family while fulfilling your duties and not remaining attached with your action at the same time. But this is the toughest thing to do," Naina said.

"There are people who are not fit in the 'samsaras',,' they also leave home," Jatin said.

"Sometimes, when your family misunderstands you and you just leave home after you tried your best to cope up with them. This happens when other people in the family are less aware and are too much materialistic. A general spiritual awareness is needed in the society."

"You believe in karma?" Jatin said.

"I believe in action, devotion, meditation, and knowledge. God is our dearest friend and guru **and that is your inner conscience.** In Mahabharata, Lord Krishna being Arjuna's friend and guru, guided him in the battlefield for fulfilling his dharma of being a Kshatriya, to fight for the right cause, to fight for the justice. Lord Krishna never took the bow and arrow in his hands on behalf of Arjuna to fight because it was Arjuna's duty."

Suresh knocked on the door. "Madam, time."

"Naina, you may keep the bottle. You said you like to drink," Jatin said, smiling.

"Really?" Naina smiled.

"Sure."

Jatin opened the door. This room was at the corner of the outside hall. There was no other customer except his friend who was sitting on the sofa, looked at Naina and smiled. Then he told Jatin, "You spent full one hour inside, what you did for so long?" He smiled wickedly.

"Went for a walk with Johnnie," Jatin said as he winked at Avinav.

Avinav looked at Naina and said, "Naina, I think you made my friend very happy."

"Ask your friend." She smiled.

"Avinav, where are Shetty and Bhatia?"

"They are still in the room, may be taking a massage," and Avinav started laughing.

Jatin shrugged his shoulder.

"Naina, sit here for some time. Make plans to come and visit our place. We will arrange hotel for you for staying. You will have real fun; you will be our guest," Avinav said.

"Really a grand idea but I don't think I will be able to go," Naina said.

"Don't worry Naina, we will pay you. You can take your friends with you. Sofia was good.

You can take Sofia or any other with whom you are comfortable."

"Thanks for the invitation. But I am comfortable here only."

"We could have gone for some outing in some resort, could have enjoyed party and long drive," Avinav said, "Think about it Naina."

"Okay, you can talk to our manager. I am sending him. You tell him about your plan."

Chapter 24

"Naina, how did you get this cut mark on your face? Exactly near your left eye?" Monica said, dipping a butter pav in her special masala tea.

Naina touched her left eye absently. It was a crazy, rainy day. All day and night, it was raining and raining. No one except Kajal and Sweety had come from outside. The insiders were sitting or lying on the beds of the rooms. Sofia, Monica, Naina, and Saloni got butter pav, samosa, and masala tea for themselves. Manilal was the person who used to run around for getting things for the ladies anytime from market.

"Life time memory," Saloni said, "A love mark from Aalok."

"Who is Aalok?" Monica asked.

"Aalok was a great person. A super hero kind of personality you will only find in films," Saloni mocked.

Naina laughed loud. "My initial days in Mumbai, I was very stupid those days."

"That's your innocence," Saloni said.

"He had stolen Naina's mother's golden jewellery," Sofia said, biting at a samosa.

"What? How come he got your mother's jewellery? Was he someone from your hometown?" Monica was inquisitive.

"He was a customer here," Naina said, sipping at her tea, "He was Saloni's customer. Saloni was going to her hometown for two months. Aalok came during that time."

"Oh okay, so both of you met here for the first time," Monica said.

"Yes, I met him in my initial days of working here," Naina said, "I could get back to my normal life only after he stole my mother's ornaments. I got my freedom in life in exchange of that gold."

"You got back to normal life? Was your life difficult with him?" Monica said.

"Her life was seriously in danger. He was such a horrible person who will get onto your nerves and make you irritated for the rest of your life," Sofia said.

"I had never met such a miser like him in my life so far," Saloni added.

"He was a fraud. He cheated his business partners," Naina said, "I didn't know that."

"Naina is too simple as a person to trust everyone. You may say anything and she will trust you," Saloni said.

"It's not that I trust everyone all the time. It's not that I believe whatever they say," Naina said, "It's just that I can't hurt people's feelings by saying something rude on their face. I can feel other's pain and that actually hurts me more."

"The miser cheater saw you spending money carelessly in that hotel for the first time when you met him outside," Saloni said.

"I really can't handle money. I had always been careless about money."

"Yes, that I have seen. You never count your money except when you need to put it in bank or need to pay somewhere. You never bargain in any shop. If I ask you how much money is there in your purse, you won't be able to say and keep everything open." Monica said.

"Actually, I am not good at calculating." She smiled.

"But how did you get so much involved with Aalok? How did everything start?" Monica asked.

"Naina met him here just once. Then they met outside in hotels," Sofia said.

"That night we had to vacate this place. Coincidentally, Aalok came that night in Mumbai.

He called me up; we met in a hotel," Naina said.

"Just one night staying and you fell in love with him?" Monica said.

"No Monica, it didn't happen in one night. It was anything but not love for sure. After he went back to his city, he kept calling and messaging me a lot. A lot means a lot. I too talked and messaged back. I couldn't be harsh on him. And that soft nature of mine created disaster and calamities in my life," Naina said.

"Tell me in little detail, Naina."

"He used to call me up and message me a lot. He said he had gone through huge losses in his business so his parents and wife insulted him. If I was not at work, I would either talk to him or chat with him.

"Though while talking over phone, I told him that I really don't like to talk, still he would insist and it happened so many times that he even held the phone without speaking anything. Still, he wanted me to be on the other side of the phone."

"My goodness! Such a chipku leech. And what about messaging?"

"As I told you if I was not at work, I would be chatting. He used to ask me who was the customer, what was his age, was he an old (known) customer or a new customer, etc. that I had to inform him from the room."

"What are you saying? This is disgusting."

"I told you I couldn't say 'no' on his face," Naina said.

"Not only him, you couldn't say anything to anyone. Always okay, yes, sure. You don't say anything rude to anyone," Saloni said.

"Not exactly, I too lose patients at time when things are just too much. And if I am angry, that's rare, then I don't know" She laughed.

"What did he do when you went for work? He must have been very impatient waiting for you?"

"Huh," Naina said, "He used to start calling me if I wouldn't have come out within thirty to forty minutes. And he kept on calling till I answered his call. And he used to do it at each and every work."

"And after that?" Monica said.

"He used to ask me what I exactly did inside the room. He used to give me instruction how to exactly do each and everything within the room. And then he used to finally cut the call after cursing the customer,"

"Oh, he lived his life at customer's money and then cursed them," Monica said.

"Yes. Aalok used to tell me to send least amount of money at my home. He used to count how much for school fees, for market, electric bill, etc. to be paid. He used to tell me to send exactly that much amount, otherwise my family would overspend. He used to count the money and keep it as well."

"But you came here for your family, right?"

"Of course, Aalok had no right to tell me where to spend, how to spend. But he was too greedy and overpowering. I was so confused not knowing how to handle things. He actually wanted to spend my money for having fun like roaming around, eating outside or on alcohol and drugs."

"Didn't he stop you from spending money on yourself?"

"Of course, he did it a lot. He didn't let me spend money on beauty parlour. He didn't let me do shopping."

"How could you tolerate so much?"

"He left his son and wife in Rajkot and came to stay with Naina in Mumbai forcefully. Naina didn't want him to do anything like this," Saloni said after pause, "Aalok has also stolen her laptop."

"So many times I have requested to leave me alone and go back to his family. But he said he would commit suicide if I leave him. And I believed he might commit suicide. He created so much mental pressure on me that you can't even imagine. He kept calling me continuously when I went to my home.

"He had taken all my contact numbers and sometimes even called them up. He kept me scared of him all the time. He made me keep his photo on my phone screen. He used to call me after I went in the room so that the customer comes to know that I already had a boyfriend."

"How did you tolerate so much?"

"You know every day he used to check my phone and listen to all the call recordings that he had set for all incoming and outgoing calls. What am I talking with the family members?

What messages some customers might have sent."

"But did you talk with customers on the phone?" Monica asked.

"You know, it was like that, they asked my number and I had just given but hardly have I talked with anybody. You know right, how less I talk," Naina said.

"But how can you work under so much of pressure?"

Naina smiled, "You don't know the worst part of my job yet, I don't think anyone had faced such a situation that I had gone through."

"What do you mean?"

"I had to call him when I was with some customer and keep the phone on in the room. He wanted to listen what I used to talk and what I used to do with customers till my job was done. And I had to do this, otherwise he used to beat me, shout at me."

"What!" Monica's mouth fell open. "Is this true?" She asked with utter surprise.

"Yes, true."

"How mean. How can someone do like this? This is the worst thing I've ever heard. And why would he want to listen what you do inside with a customer? You do your job inside. Why is he bothered?"

"He wanted to keep a check on me and keep me scared and watched."

"How was your physical relation with him?"

"He was too much into physical things. He used to force me to be physical. He even used to call up my friends."

"Yes," Saloni said, "Sweety was telling me the same thing. After doing drugs, Aalok called her up. He even called Manisha."

"My God."

"Shouting, screaming and nagging was what he did all the time," Naina said, "I don't know Monica how to explain to you. He kept calling me continuously and shouted so much on me regarding my service and everything that it kept me panicky all the time. He always used to doubt that I am having some secret affair with someone."

"I thought how come an educated girl like you went in his hands. He is the most horrible, dangerous and miser leech I have ever met in my life," Saloni said.

"He talked sweetly at the beginning and Naina got carried away. What else?" Sofia said.

"That was there, as you said he talked sweetly. He told me about his loses in the business and how he suffered for that," Naina said, "He said how badly he is disturbed in his family life.

And I felt sympathy for him. I couldn't understand his motive behind telling me all this. Later, I realised that he actually wanted to gain my sympathy."

"Naturally," said Sofia, "You paid the hotel bill when he came here and you stayed back in the night. He understood he can easily use your money."

"But how and when did he steal your mother's ornaments?" Monica said.

"I had got the gold from Calcutta, for giving into mortgage. I had paid the deposit and had purchased things for my rented room with that money. It took more than one and half year to pay back the loan with interest. When I got the gold back, Aalok came. He stayed back in the night. While going in the morning, he took the gold with him."

Everyone fell silent in the room. Monica broke the silence by asking, "How could you simply leave him? You could have gone to the police, right?"

"No, I didn't. I simply went back to Calcutta. I knew he might start his business using my mother's jewellery. Let him do it. At least he would be on the right path and let me live in peace."

"What kind of a man is he? I am not getting any suitable word to describe him," Monica said.

"You know, once he had beaten Naina in a hotel room for two days?" Saloni said.

"What!"

"Yes, she was being beaten for two days and when she was back at this place, her whole body had black marks."

"But how come he could beat you for two days? Naina, you could have come out from the room."

"How could I ? He was either shouting or beating me. We were doing drugs. Later when he Became high, he started shouting and screaming."

"And what were you doing when he was beating you?"

"I was simply looking at him and watching him beating and shouting. What much could I do?" Naina said and laughed.

Monica broke out into laughter. She tried to compose herself. "How can you be so cool?"

Monica said, after calming herself down.

"Not all the time I used to remain cool. I too shouted. Mostly out of frustration. I wanted to get away from him. But he was not ready to leave me and go at any cost. He was after me and with me like a parasite on a tree for its nutrition. And I was getting suffocated like I was being strangulated.

"From the morning till night, he used to ask me each and everything in detail. When I went for a night job, he used to call me. Every time before going for work, he used to say to be very careful. I mean, you can't imagine. I used to ask him to be very careful for what? Was I going to fight a battle?"

They burst into laughter.

"He even called up at my home and family people and said all bad things about me. He had used so many bad words about me that you cannot even think. He called up the customers and said all bad things about me," Naina said after some time.

Chapter 25

"Do you know what happened to Jiya? She is not coming from the last two weeks. She is not even picking up any call. I am worried for her," Veena asked Shweta.

Shweta was applying nail polish on her nails. She looked up at Veena. "No Madam, I don't have any idea. You can ask Vinay ji; he has all the news of Jiya. She gives him so many customers," Shweta said and focused on applying nail paint again.

Saloni said, "She must have gone somewhere with some customer. She knows many of them personally."

Sofia said, "She was telling me that she might go to Lonavala."

"When did she tell you? I am worried about her health. She takes too much MD. She has many drug addict customers too." Veena was a bit tensed.

"I heard her talking with someone over phone about hotel bookings in Lonavala. Later, she was telling me that she might go there for a few days," Sofia said.

They were sitting in Veena's room in the afternoon. They didn't eat lunch because that day was Tina's son's fifth birthday. She was giving them a treat. Ladies who used to come from outside normally would be here after five pm. Only few people used to stay there day and night including Naina, Shweta, Sofia, Saloni, and Tina were present then.

Tina had already ordered chicken biryani in 'Delhi Durbar' for them and vegetable biryani for Naina. The food was on the way.

Sarah went to the market yesterday; they gave hermoney to get something nice for her son. Sarah got a nice wrist watch. Tina liked it very much.

Shweta said, "Remember Madam, Prashant used to come here often and spent day and night till his account used to be empty."

"I know, I remember very well," Saloni said, "Prashant was a regular customer of Natasha. Natasha told me how Prashant used to watch pornography, doing drugs all day and night continuously without stopping. After sometimes, he used to take other women."

I mean, seriously, can you imagine someone watching pornography for hours and hours, days after days?"

"Watching pornography and taking continuous service of multiple women, this is what I have seen people doing here after drugs."

"Where is Prashant nowadays? He doesn't come here anymore," Shweta enquired.

"Good that he doesn't come here anymore. He used to give his gold chains, rings to manager and tell to get him more stuff," Veena said.

"Natasha helped him with money," Saloni said.

"Later Prashant stopped coming here, started calling Natasha directly in his house. He was living alone. Natasha shifted to Prashant's place. She stopped working here," Veena said.

"Then what happened, did he marry her and got settled in life?" Naina asked her.

"Marriage? Forget it, Prashant was totally into drugs. He was living in a rented small room; he spent all his savings, sold his flat and car for drugs," Saloni said.

"And what happened to Natasha?" Naina said.

"He kept Natasha for a few months with him. You know how things go after drugs. Natasha sold her jewellery to buy drugs for him. He went more into drugs."

"This happens with drug addiction. Remember Mayank, how was he?" Veena said.

"How can we forget him? He used to come in the evening around six and then used to take girls one after one. Sometimes, he used to be with the same girl for two-three days,"

Shweta said. "Drug addict people want only such girls who would take drugs with them. Initially, girls

take drugs for giving service to get customers and later, they become drug addicts and waste their money and health after drugs," Saloni said.

"Saloni, you remember how Mayank used to stay here for two days, three days or for a week for taking drugs and girls." Sofia said.

"Kavya encouraged him to take drugs. He drank alcohol but he was never into drugs. But when Kavya met him, she gave him drugs for the first time."

"I know, Sanjay ji was telling one day," Tina said, "Mayank started asking girls on credit. He gave him credit for a few days. Then he too stopped giving him credit. When Sanjay stopped giving him credit, then Mayank started calling all his friends asking for money. Fewbof them gave him money; he again got drugs and girls with that money. Later, his friends too stopped giving him money."

"Mayank's life got spoilt due to Kavya," Saloni said, irritated.

"Some girls get addicted to drugs and then they make the customers drug addicts to get continuous supply of drugs," Naina said.

Babloo called from outside, "Tina madam, your biryani order has reached. Shall I get it here or will you all go to the kitchen?"

Veena said, "We will have it here, you give us the parcels and few plates and spoons."

Babloo gave them the packets. There were some other food and desserts too. They ate in silence. "How is your son celebrating his birthday?" Naina asked, while washing hands.

Tina used to look so bright when she used to talk about her son. She said, "In our village, we don't celebrate birthdays but my Maa cooked rice and milk kheer and other special dishes for him. My sister and her son also live in the same house. I believe they are having a good time together."

Along with her own family, Tina took care of her sister's family too. Her sister's husband died in a road accident, after a few years their child was born. Tina would do everything for her sister's family as long as she could.

Naina said, "Madam, do you have any happy story where a woman and a customer got married and are happy in their life?"

"Yes, there was a girl named Ayesha. She got married to Ravi. He had a business of gold jewellery. She never came back in this place. Hopefully, she is doing fine. Actually Naina, girls who come here, they all have financial problems. They come for earning money. Customers come to a prostitute to ejaculate, they don't love."

"Madam, what I have seen in the past few years is that mostly the idea of love is only associated with the physical body and material gain. We love each other till we are interested in each other's body and till we get profit from each other. Love fades away as soon as bodily attraction goes away. This is not love. This is desire for physical intimacy and material gain. Attraction becomes our desire; we think this desire is love.

"True love is not about body, status, name, or fame like illusionary things. True love is having trust and faith in each other and it is about the sacrifices we make for each other. True love is about understanding each other. True love is practising spirituality together. We need to sacrifice our mundane negative desires for each other in love.

"Sometimes, we meet some people in our life and feel, as if we know this person from long back, we get this feeling due to our strong, past life, soul connection of many birth times. Nowadays, our mind is attached with worldly physical materialistic matter more, so our mindis unaware. So naturally, we get confused within desire and love."

Veena said, "Naina, you keep watching YouTube. Do you learn such knowledge from YouTube?"

She smiled. "I listen to a lot of music including mantra chanting, Sufi songs, bhajans and Hindi film songs. I watch spiritual videos, motivational videos to learn about life and spirituality. These are self-realised feelings."

"Our birth is a curse," Veena said, "Life of a woman is full of suffering and pain. Women are being exploited massively. Already girl child is unwanted in many families. We don't want to educate girls because ultimately, she will go to someone else's house.

"So, educating girls is a bad investment in such a family where income is less. But boys need to be educated well because they will take responsibilities. For marriage purpose also, parents of a girl need to arrange a huge amount of money as dowry. That is again a problem."

"You are right, Madam. we often neglect a girl's education; we don't realise how important it is to educate the girls. Girls become mothers and mothers should be well educated to raise children with proper guidance. Mother is the first guru at home from whom we get the 'Samskaras',,' learn the culture. Our nature of the present life gets a direction.

"If we see from the astrological point of view, Jupiter is the guru. Guru takes us from darkness to light. Jupiter signifies higher knowledge, wisdom, Dharma, luck, happiness. It gets exalted in the sign of Cancer in the fourth house of the Kalpurusha chart. Fourth house and Cancer sign both signifies home, mother, homely comforts. When we don't get our mother at home as our guru, our base is weak. We lack love and affection when mother is not at home.

"In the Kalpurusha basic chart, ninth house is house of father, Dharma, higher knowledge, guru, luck. Sign Sagittarius falls there which is mool trikona, sign of Jupiter. So, in the form of mother and father, we get our luck, Dharma, and guru in the present lifetime.

"The education which we get at school doesn't remove our inner darkness. Without spiritual knowledge our learning is incomplete. Without spiritual knowledge we never grow in life, only the physical body grows with age.

"The education which we get in schools, teaches us to be competitive and money minded. If our son or daughter comes first in class, then they will be appreciated, otherwise their study and career is gone. This learning process is making them jealous, angry, proudproud, and negative.

"Education is making them be professional without professional ethics. Somehow, people are just trying to achieve success even at the cost of others pain and suffering sometimes. Thus, they entangle themselves more into karma to be paid back.

"In our family, we raise male child and female child differently. Women do all the works of a house and pamper the male child. The male child doesn't learn day to day house work. Man thinks he is born superior to the woman, so he should be served. Man doesn't learn to respect woman in such environment.

"We all should divide house work within all the family members, most importantly we should learn to do our own work, irrespective of gender. The problem is in the base, it creates a thought that who earns money, is the superior. The whole concept of child rising is revolving around earning money. So, the primary focus of our life becomes money. Thus, we lower our consciousness and remain in sorrows,"

"We only talk and discuss so many things but ultimately nothing changes. We remain in the darkness throughout our life," Tina said.

"Because we are not united, we hate people and create division. We pay attention in fighting and finding faults in people. We don't think of helping each other and growing together,"

"For that we need to learn to appreciate first," Sofia said.

"Most importantly, we need education for all," Naina said.

Chapter 26

Naina and Saloni were walking along the corridor when Anika was coming from the opposite side. She almost shouted, "Hey, be careful, don't touch me."

"What happened?" Naina asked.

"I just had a bath. I am going in the lounge for praying."

In the lounge, there was a very small wooden temple fixed on the wall. Few God's idols were kept there to be worshipped every day. Anika used to come from Mira Road. Last night, she was busy with a full night customer here, so she couldn't go home. After taking a bath, she was going there for praying.

"If we touch you, will you be dirty? So, are we dirty?" Saloni asked.

Anika looked irritated, she said, "Don't you see Saloni, every time after giving service I take bath at the bathroom that is there in the hall outside. I maintain my cleanliness. But you all take bath within the room bathroom."

"So, does it make you cleaner?" Saloni said.

"Whatever, I don't want to be touched before my prayer," Anika said, voice firm.

"Well, Anika," Naina said, "The water used in your bath is full of small dust particles and germs. If you don't believe, see through a microscope. The air in which we all are breathing is full of dust or germs particles. The floor on which you are walking on is full of dust. No matter however and how many times we clean, still every moment, everywhere there is avlayer of dust flowing in the air, especially when the air of our country is so polluted.

"As soon as you clean it, again dust is flowing on it. Dust is our earth element with which you are made, I am made, she is made, he is made and animals are made. Whom do you think you are avoiding?"

"Why do we take a bath? We should remain dirty all our life because every time dust is falling on us," Anika said.

Naina smiled. "We need to take a bath every day to maintain a standard cleanliness so that the dust particles and germs don't get accumulated on skin to make us fall sick," she said,

"After taking a bath, you feel clean from inside. It gives you freshness. It makes you energetic. That does not mean you stop touching other people before you worship God.

"The most important thing is your mind should be clean from all the barriers and limitations of such small petty thoughts which hold you back and don't let you grow to look beyond your limitations. Can you limit God within the idol? He is infinite. God is everywhere and within everyone. Just you are unaware."

"I don't know all this. My daughter has her final exam tomorrow. I have to give her a flower from the God's garland. She will keep it in her purse. So, I have to be very clean before I touch God," Anika said, while maintaining a safe distance from Naina and Saloni.

"On the idol of the God, dust is flowing too. The air that is touching you, also touches the idol of the God. When you have right knowledge, then you keep God in clean mind, naturally you act right. Your right action makes you give good exam. When you keep God out of your mind, you hate people, divide people, behave in wrong manner with the people, animals and create negativity all around you," Naina said.

"Anika," said Saloni, "You will keep the flower in the purse, which is full of dust. You will walk on the road, which is full of dust. People urinate on the road, they spit. Mostly, the drains are open. Dustbins on the roads are overflowing. Air is passing on all of these open drains, urine, garbage, etc. and touching us as well as your flower. Point to think."

Naina added, "We breathe through our nostrils, which is full of dust and mucus. We pass air from our body which gets mixed in the air in which we all breathe and eat. In the deep forest or in caves of Himalayas where the yogis or saints stay and do spiritual practices, they may not take a bath every day.

"Think about our body; on the skin, we have dead cells, dust. Just below the skin we have blood, mucus, saliva, undigested food, urine, and stool. These are always within our body; we are moving around carrying all these all the time. Everything is just packed from outside by the skin. Open the skin and keep it like that just for one day, body will start to rot because body is physical, mortal and perishable," Naina said.

"So, the idea of cleanliness for worshipping God is in our mind. We need to clean our mind first from selfishness, greed, envy, anger, lust, and limitations," Saloni said.

"I never thought this way because we were never taught to think this way," Anika said.

"Anika, did you have 'Gita' at your home? Or the Ramayana? Mahabharata?"

"No, I didn't see them at my home."

"So how did you learn the way of living if not from 'Gita'?"

"I have learnt from my elders and I am passing the same knowledge and values ahead."

"What all have you learnt?"

"I learnt that I have to study well to get good marks to get a good job for earning money and well settled life. I learnt not to give anything to anyone. I learnt to hide my feelings from others, otherwise people will take my advantage. I learnt if I don't make the other person a fool, he/she will make me a fool.

"I learnt to prove I am always better than the other person. I learnt to find faults in others to prove my superiority. I learnt that I should always get more than the other person. I learnt to ask for job, marriage or house from God. I learnt to be proud for doing anything good. I learnt to hate the poor and to flatter the rich.

"I learnt to manipulate people for fulfilling my selfish desire. I learnt to take advantage of simple people's simplicity and kind people's kindness. I learnt to fulfil my own desire by any means. I learnt to save my own money like a miser but when I get to spend other people's money, I spend lavishly."

"And after all these, you go and pray to God with a clean body?"

"Did you learn how to be humble?" Saloni asked.

"No, I have learnt to be proud of my achievements."

"And what is the idea of your achievement?"

"It is all about the money and position in the society so that I can show off to all and be proud of myself."

"Hmm!"

Saloni and Naina exchanged smiles. Naina said, "This is not our fault. This is Kaliyug, you see."

Chapter 27

Chintu was stirring boiling tea with a big spoon. Nice aroma of the tea filled the inside hall room. Naina said, "Chintu, please give us tea, is your tea ready?"

"Madam, please wait for a few minutes. It is boiling."

"Okay."

Zarina took out a packet of biscuits from her purse. Sofia took out an apple from her bag.

Naina took out some dry fruits on a plate. While chewing some almonds, she thought of doing make-up. She never did much make-up. She loved to put kajal and eyeliner, making them dark on her eyes and then some lipstick.

She was thinking which lipstick to put! There were light pink, mauve, red, orange, copper and maroon. She was wearing black shorts, so she thought of wearing red lipstick. Just then Chintu gave her tea. She put the lipstick back in her purse.

"Thank you, Chintu. I was waiting for it," she said as she sipped at the steaming hot tea.

He smiled in return. Nafisa was talking with her boyfriend over the phone. After her talk was over, she said, "Shamim's mother is not well, she has got stones in kidneys."

"What did the doctor say?" Naina asked.

"Doctor said to go for an operation," Nafisa said, "I may have to help him with some money."

"Hey girls, come to this side of the hall," Vinay called them.

Two people in their thirties were staring at the ladies quietly. After some time, one of them pointed at Nafisa. She went inside. The other person was confused from the start itself, as if he was thinking whether to take any girl or not.

"Sir, make choice please, ladies are standing," Vinay said.

"You let them go, I will say later," he said.

"Thank you girls, go inside."

"How will he choose? He does not get an erection," Simran said after they came back and sat inside the hall.

"How do you know that?" Naina asked.

"I know because I had spent two hours with him here. That night, I didn't get any work till two o'clock. I was worried; I was praying at least I should get one work. Then Vinay ji sent me with this guy. He told me to take special care of him.

"I went inside the room. He was drunk, not getting an erection at all even after giving my best. Still, he was trying every possible way to get that hard. I tried my best in every possible way. Later I requested him to leave me, to let me go. I almost cried inside but he was telling that he needed to be a man because his parents want him to get married immediately. So, he was desperate. Later, I felt bad for him but that night was horrible," Simran said.

"Parents are not free with their son and daughter; they are not their friends. Thus, they find friendship outside and discuss all their personal matters with their friends only. They also belong to their age. What more can they say. The solution that comes out from this discussion you can easily guess," Naina said.

"We meet the outcome of such discussion here at this brothel." Monica said.

"Just think how limited and conservative is our thought and idea about being a man or a woman. Our thought is limited within our sense organs only. A man needs to prove himself by his erection and a woman needs to prove herself by her virginity. Our whole consciousness is limited within our basic sensual needs." Saloni said.

Naina said, "Man and woman are identified by sex organs of course, but the soul inside them is greater than their identity of being a man, woman, or transgender. We must respect people, irrespective of their gender. We all are doing our own respective karma in the universe related to our gender, cast, race, family or job whatever.

"There is no point in hating or disrespecting people. The soul present within our subtle body is one for all. The subtle body is carrying all the identities from previous lives. All the five elements are same within every one's body. The existing consciousness is also eternal and unchanging for all.

"But the intelligence cannot reflect similar consciousness within us because our subtle and gross body both are physical and bound with karma, so we have limitation of thoughts, ideas and knowledge. Lord Krishna says in the Gita to do one's own duty or to live one's own dharma meaning doing Swadharma.

"Lord Krishna is the supreme almighty, the eternal consciousness bliss. 'Gita' and astrology are the supreme knowledge of spirituality. When we become a devotee of Lord Krishna, read 'Gita', study Astrology and understand karma, then we realise the truth and proceed in the path of liberation by removing ignorance **and realising the self.**"

"But you said everything is predestined."

"Destiny and free will are two sides of the same coin. Destiny is absolute truth and free will is illusionary truth at the physical level of Maya. I have explained both. Now, it's up to you."

www.ingramcontent.com/pod-product-compliance
Lightning Source LLC
LaVergne TN
LVHW091630070526
838199LV00044B/1006